Awaken Your Spirit!

Lift the Veil and Receive the Light!

Awaken Your Spirit!

Lift the Veil and Receive the Light!

Edward N Brown

Crystal Sea Press
Chicago, Illinois

AWAKEN YOUR SPIRIT!
Lift the Veil and Receive the Light!

ISBN: 978-1-7367712-8-0
Library of Congress Control Number: 2023937384

Published by Crystal Sea Press
Chicago, IL
Printed in the United States of America
CSP
For information about this title, or to order other books and/or electronic media, contact the publisher at: http://www.crystalseapress.com

Notice

This is a Christian oriented book, but not all Christians believe all the same things – especially regarding design, creation, and functionality of life and nature. And differing opinions can sometimes be quite intransigent. But no person's viewpoint should be summarily dismissed, regardless of how unreasonable it may sound to you. The truth of the matter is that when discussing philosophy and religion, the concepts involved are mostly beyond our finite ability to comprehend them. So, patience, humility, and compassion are extremely important. The material in this book is solely the personal viewpoint of the author – no religious denomination is defended or opposed. The only assumed tenet is belief in the one, true, Christian triune God. Although this precept is itself debatable, that is the subject of a separate exercise for another time. If you do not believe in God – or have other rigid theological beliefs — then you are free to ignore this text. But if you are open-minded and not sure about all the details, then please read on. It's not too long. And don't forget to read the endnotes and the Appendices somewhere along the way – you'll be glad you did.

Edward N Brown
February 2023

Credits:

Front Cover image of an angel –
	by Evelyn deMorgan
Copyright: Released by Karen Arnold under license CC0, Public Domain
Title: "The Storm Spirits showing angels and spirits causing chaos and turbulence of rain, thunder and lightning"
Medium: vintage art painting
filename: angels-spirits-vintage-art.jpg
Access: https://www.publicdomainpictures.net/en/free-download.php?image=evelyn-de-morgan-vintage-art&id=455267

Front Cover image of a head and brain –
Free to use under the Content License - (no attribution required)
filename: understanding-gd5d894b0e_1920.jpg

Back Cover image of a head and brain –
Free to use under the Content License - (no attribution required)
filename: quantum-physics-g2b90c7ad2_1920.jpg

CONTENTS

INTRODUCTION

Tired of looking for those miracles you hear so much about? Frustrated that you've never seen or encountered a miracle yourself? You know that some people say that there is no such thing as miracles – that everything can be explained by science. You want to believe in miracles, but you have lingering doubts. Well, relax – take a deep breath. The best example of a miracle is not in some strange faraway place in Portugal, Mexico, or France.[1] Yes, the majesty of the cosmos, the planet earth, and the life all about us is a great miracle. But the greatest miracle – and the one closest to your very being – is right inside your very self – the human spirit inside your very soul. You can pretend that it doesn't exist, but the more you try, the more troubled you become. The existence of the human spirit – the creation of your spirit – is a miracle that cannot be ignored or explained away by clever reasoning. The proof is right inside you, and you know it. No need to turn to strange gurus or distant shrines. Just listen to your heart.[2]

You are a human being. You have a soul and a spirit – or so you think. But do you really? You'll get different answers if you talk to different people or read different things. And it can be very confusing.

But now you have picked up this book. You're wondering if it's any good – does it have any answers that you feel comfortable with? So, dear reader, at the very outset, here is the gist of it:

You **DO** possess an advanced rational soul and an immortal activated ethereal spirit.[3] However, the bad news is that your spirit is veiled. The good news is that you can control the position of the veil by your own willpower.

Why would you want to do this? Because by unveiling your spirit, you invite the presence of the Holy Spirit to infuse into your being. You can receive the divine gifts of sanctification, salvation, and eternal life. You can be together with your loved ones, and the holy family of God forever.

There's just one catch. Satan can also enter into your spirit. And he will try every trick in the book to corrupt your willpower. And his lures may look very enticing in this earthly realm. You see, he wants you to be at his footstool, not the other way around.

Of course, there are a lot of gory details about all this. And you probably have questions. So, that's where this book comes in. You may find your answers here – or you may not. But hey, you will find lots of interesting information – stuff definitely worth mulling over!

NOTES

1 The shrines of Our Lady of Fatima in Portugal, Our Lady of Guadalupe in Mexico, and Our Lady of Lourdes in France are three of the best-known Marian apparition sites where the miracle of an appearance of the Blessed Virgin Mary is said to have occurred.

2. The pop song by Roxette notwithstanding, 'listening to your heart' is a common expression that derives from Psychology. Instead of listening to a little voice from inside our heads, it is often recommended that we listen to the voice from inside our hearts. It's part of something called interoception, a cognitive-affective process of how well individuals can perceive subtle bodily changes. It is thought that bodily signals from the heart offer good guidance about potential choices.

Among the ancient Hebrews, the heart was regarded not only as the seat of the passions and emotions (love, pleasure, grief, hatred), but also of the intellectual faculties (thought and understanding). Therefore, in the Bible (Refer to Matthew 9:4), the heart is often represented as the center of man's moral and spiritual actions, and as the seat of corruption caused by sin. **In reality, the heart is a window for glimpsing into the soul and spirit.** Refer to Proverbs 4:23: *Watch over your heart with all diligence, for from it flow the springs of life.*

3. The soul is the vital principle by which the body is animated. Without the soul, the body is dead. It is rational because it follows the God-given laws of nature. The spirit is the vital principle by which a person feels, thinks, and wills in opposition to the flesh. It is ethereal because it is invisibly embedded within the soul.

Don't be confused when Bible translations indicate that Jesus said *"Blessed are the poor in spirit"* in the first of the Beatitudes at the Sermon on the Mount (Matthew 5:3). This verse must be carefully taken in the proper context. What 'those who are 'poor in spirit' actually means is 'those who know themselves to be spiritually lacking in godliness – who recognize that they are incapable of providing for themselves spiritually by their own strength, goodness, or righteousness – who realize their own spiritual shortcomings and their unequivocal need for Him'. Indeed, the kingdom of heaven will be populated by the humble and not the arrogant – those who recognize their need for a savior. In that way, the 'poor in spirit' are blessed.

1 – THE DIVINE REALITY

First, we need to put forward the two cornerstones of the big picture:

1) The Great Existence is the infinite and eternal spirit realm of Divine Reality.

2) The Great Existent is the invisible triune God of pure divine spirit – omnipotent, omniscient, omnipresent, eternal, and immutable; the essence of Truth and Love.[1]

At some point within the infinite and eternal spirit realm of Divine Reality, God created other entities – 'objects', simple and complex 'creatures', and other 'beings' with consciousness, sentience, and sapience (including reason, understanding, and will).[2] This is the greatest of all mysteries.

At first, God created spirit entities within this spirit realm [3]– spirit-beings (such as angels, the heavenly host, elders, and witnesses),[4] spirit-creatures (such as the 'living creatures' and horses),[5] spirit-florae (the garden of God),[6] and spirit-objects (such as thrones, crowns, robes, altars, trumpets, torches, jewels, seals/scrolls, harps, and vessels).[7] We don't know the order of creation, and we don't know the exact composition of these spirit-things since our comprehension of the essence of 'spirit' is just too limited.[8]

Thereafter, God created a new and different parallel space/time realm in a progressive unfolding manner (evolving), composed of non-spirit entities, corporeal in nature and comprised of physical matter/energy and data/information. The creation of corporeal-objects (with a non-living chemistry, such as gas/liquid/solid articles), corporeal-primitives (rudimentary organisms with a living chemistry), and corporeal-creatures (organisms with a living chemistry [9]– a life-force called a 'soul')[10] followed in due time in an evolutionary manner.

Finally, in a glorious crowning achievement, God created a united spiritual/corporeal being, composed of both spirit and non-spirit corporeality with a soul. This being, with body, soul, and spirit is us – the human being, the highest level of animal – one with consciousness, sentience, and sapience. The spirit-portion of this being was created similar to the other spirit-only beings, the angels. The non-spirit corporeal portion was created in the mind of God to be a reflection of His glorious majesty. However, the body, soul, and even the spirit, are bounded by physical limitations of corporeality (finite matter, energy, and information). The similarity and reflection are true, but quantitatively how true, is known only to God. Consequently, it is said that we are made in the 'image of God', so to speak. Again, this is a great mystery.

NOTES

1. The Great Existent is called Yahweh or Jehovah (He who exists) by the ancient Hebrews, the first formal societal group to embrace the concept of incorporeal monotheism (the Egyptian era of Atenism excluded). God's name was so holy that it was impious to say it aloud. The official designation was YHWH or JHVH – the tetragrammaton (the 4-letter name of God). In Judaism, it's now common to refer to God by the titular names 'Elohim' or 'Adonai'. In the Bible, when the word **LORD** is in all capitals, it usually means the tetragrammaton. In the Old Testament, God reveals Himself as 'I AM THAT I AM' (or 'I AM WHO I AM').

2. Sapience is the cognitive basis for judgment, moral sentiment, strategic thinking, and system perspective – it integrates emotions, moral/social drives, intelligent decision-making, and creativity.

3. The first created entities existed only in the realm of spirit. An interesting topic within the field of metaphysics is the study of the spirit realm (what it is composed of, and the laws under which it functions), from the highest heaven at the highest level to the lowest hell at the lowest level. 3, 7, and 12 levels of heaven have been postulated by various philosophers; and 7, 9, and 10 levels of hell have been suggested [the non-biblical work *The Inferno*, by Dante, gives 9 levels]. Much of what we think we know about Heaven comes from the Book of Revelation, which is written in a dreamlike, figurative language. Consequently, it's difficult to discern what may be metaphorical and what may be literal.

4. Note that Lucifer (or Satan) and the other fallen angels (demons, devils) are also spirit-beings created by God prior to the creation of the Earth [and possibly prior to creation of our corporeal universe]. They were created in a state of 100% Goodness, but by their own willful free choice, have lost all of that Goodness and have become 0% Good (or 100% Bad, or 'evil'). Because they are spirit-only, their fallen state is unchangeable and unforgiveable by God. Their fate is eternal damnation and separation from God.

Little is known about the elders and witnesses (may be resurrected disciples and prophets), who only appear in the Book of Revelation

(Revelation 4, 5, 11). Whether they are of the same 'stuff' as angels is uncertain.

5. 'creatures' here meaning spirit forms equivalent to corporeal life forms at a level lower than that of a 'being'. For example, the 'living creatures' of Revelation 4 and the horses of Revelation 6.

6. Revelation 2:7

7. 'objects' exist in the heavenly city, the house of many mansions (Reference: John 14:1-3, Revelation 4, 8). Also note the story in Revelation 21 where a new Jerusalem, the holy city, comes down to earth out of heaven.

8. Some philosophers suspect that the spiritual realm is composed of many different levels of spiritual space/time, spiritual matter/energy, and spiritual data/information. The spirit-matter and spirit-energy aspects may be thought to be analogous to the physical matter and energy components in the corporeal realm. It is also likely that there is a spirit-data and spirit-information aspect that is akin to the concepts of data and information in the corporeal realm. Note that 'spirit' is often referred to as just 'spirit-energy'.

9. 'organism' is the broad term for an individual biological life-form on Earth. Organisms are classified into Archaea, Bacteria, or Eukarya – plants, fungi, and animals being in Eukarya, with animals at the highest level. Consult any good Biology text for more insights into the 'hierarchy of life', the 'levels of organization', and the 'classification' (taxonomy) of organic structures.

It is theoretically possible that organisms could exist on other planets or moons if it is in God's creative plan. The planets Venus and Mars, and the outer moons Europa and Enceladus, are prime candidates. But a subject of more interest and theological debate is whether human being-like creatures, or creatures composed of both spirit and corporeality in the 'image of God' (or maybe not in His image, but a different image?) could exist on other planets – and if so, how similar to us would they be? Although possible, it's unlikely that this question will be answered in the near future. Within our solar system, because of the extremely unfavorable environmental conditions involved, the probability is near zero.

Within our galaxy, and all the other galaxies in the universe, the question is open. However, the distances are so vast and the time lags are so long (even at the speed of light) that exploratory probes become almost untenable. The Search for Extraterrestrial Intelligence (SETI) approach is our best hope of answering this question at this point in our history, but even that approach is low probability.

10. The level of sophistication and complexity within a soul ranges from the ultra-primitive found in simple life forms, to the advanced multifaceted and intricate soul of the human being.

2 – BODY, SOUL, AND SPIRIT

In the human being, there are three distinguishable functionalities, although they cannot be separated into distinct parts like in a machine: 1) the material body (the physical aspect); 2) the invisible soul (the life force, vitality aspect, inner-self, or essence of life); and 3) the ethereal spirit (the God-centered or divine aspect).[1]

A computer system can be a useful analogy. Think of the body as the hardware (processor, memory, input/output interface, power supply, etc.), the soul as the central operating system software (like Windows® or Android®), and the spirit as application program software (like the 'Phone' or 'Messages' app) that provides communication and interaction with the one true God. More on this later.

Plants and fungi have a body and a proto-soul.[2] Animals have a body and a primitive soul (they are capable of relating to humans and to other animals). Humanoids living prior to Adam and Eve, or not directly descended from Adam and Eve, have a body, a more advanced soul, and a primitive spirit. Human beings descended from Adam and Eve, have a God-given higher advanced soul and a God-given activated spirit (known as spiritual vigor).[3]

The body touches the material world through the five senses of sight, smell, hearing, taste, and touch. Sensory data flows to the processors in the soul, resulting in imagination, conscience, memory, reason, and the 'affections'. The spirit receives processed data (impressions) from the soul (both material and emotive in nature), and processes them further, resulting in the mystical passions of faith, hope, reverence, prayer, and worship.[4]

THE NATURE OF SOUL AND SPIRIT

The soul and the spirit have often been intermingled. While not altogether incorrect, for the purpose of clarity of thought, it's probably best to keep them separate. Both in Greek and in Hebrew, soul and spirit are distinguished by different words (*psyche* vs. *pneuma* in Greek – *nephesh* vs. *ruach* in Hebrew).

The Bible also seems to distinguish three functionalities of the complete person. For example, Saint Paul prays to God for sanctification of the people of his church in preparation for the Lord's coming:

May the God of peace make you perfect in holiness. May he preserve you whole and entire – spirit, soul, and body, irreproachable at the coming of our Lord Jesus Christ. – 1 Thessalonians 5:23

The author of the Epistle to the Hebrews also provides an example:

Indeed, God's word is living and effective, sharper than any two-edged sword. It penetrates and divides soul and spirit, joints and marrow; it judges the reflections and thoughts of the heart. – Hebrews 4:12

However, it should be understood that the nature of the human being is holistic – he/she should be understood as an integrated whole rather the sum of various separate parts. The entire human body shares in the dignity of the 'image of God': It is precisely because it is infused with a soul and a spirit, that a living creature becomes a human being and not just an animal. The human person, created in the image of God, and **WILLED** by God, is a being at once corporeal and spiritual.

The human body is an integral element of 'conscious spiritual existence' – a spirit-filled organic entity – which emerges from a composite whole being comprised of body, soul, and spirit.[5] The human body is a spiritualized material entity precisely because it is enlivened by a soul and a spirit. Though made of body, soul, and spirit, the human being is an integrated unity.

The unity of body, soul, and spirit is so profound that one has to consider the soul and spirit to be the 'structural form' of the body. It is because of the soul and spirit, that the body, made of living matter, transforms into a human being. There are not three natures united, but rather the integrated union forms a single nature.

WHAT THE SPIRIT IS NOT

The human spirit is a key element in the studies of philosophy, psychology, curative health, and religion. It is also a popular focus for shoddy practitioners of fringe therapeutic and self-help shams and charades. That is because many people have been led to believe that the human spirit is associated with an impersonal energy of some kind.

Many proponents of progressive, trendy, or new-age fads believe that a god is the source of an impersonal and universal energy that permeates the universe – a particular extension or component of the cosmos. In this sense, many believe that this god is the life force of the world. As such, they believe that the human spirit is the impersonal higher component of human nature, that is itself part of a universal oneness or life force – part of the overall universal energy.

According to the National Institutes for Health, there are currently more than 60 healing techniques that are based on the alleged existence of a universal life force or energy which permeates all of creation.[6] These practices include Reiki, yoga, acupuncture, therapeutic touch (Healing Touch, Hands of Light, etc.), tai chi, reflexology, Qi Gong, polarity therapy, and a host of others.

This energy is in the form of waves (like radio waves) or fields (like the magnetic field around a bar magnet). Workers in these disciplines believe that illness occurs when this energy becomes unbalanced, and that they can restore this balance by manipulating or channeling it in one fashion or another.

In spite of a complete lack of scientific evidence, these 'energy healing' and 'spiritual medicine' techniques have become very prevalent in U.S. health care. Every day in the U.S., many healthcare workers who are dabbling in these marginal alternative practices, routinely walk into hospital rooms and employ unregulated and scientifically unsubstantiated treatments.

But neither this hypothetical energy, or the therapeutic effects of manipulating it, have been demonstrated convincingly by any biophysical means. Furthermore, these techniques can actually be dangerous if a person suffering from a serious disease forgoes conventional medicine for any of these forms of healing.[7]

Confusion among the public is exacerbated by mock healing practitioners who hype-up the kind of energy being manipulated. Some use terms such as 'vital force' or 'bioenergetic', which sounds cool but can mean just about anything. [8]

Compounding the problem are attempts by unethical practitioners to apply a Christian veneer to these practices to make them more palatable to the faithful. For instance, some practitioners claim that Jesus may have used Reiki, or claim that the energy they are manipulating is actually the Holy Spirit. Others say that the source of the energy is the 'essence of God'.

But it's all claptrap – utter nonsense. The concept of this universal energy is not a Christian belief – it is a thoroughly new-age concept, dreamed up by secular mystics and promulgated by money-driven swindlers and con-artists.

Fake 'energy healers' also like to refer to the Christian practice of 'laying on of hands' as a sign that Jesus either used (or was channeling) some kind of energy force when He healed people. But this is not true. The Christian 'laying on of hands' in healing has nothing to do with the channeling of energy. It is just a visual representation of one person interceding with God for another. The healing is because of faith.

The Christian understanding is that God is the maker of heaven and earth, and the source of all personal life. God is Himself personal (as Father, Son, and Holy Spirit). He created the universe in order to personally share His divine life with His created corporeal creatures. The human being, in the 'image of God', is a union of body, soul, and spirit – each aspect being an essential form of the overall entity.[9] The spirit is **NOT** an energy force.

In reality, it is the soul that is the life-principle of the body, not something else. The spirit is that aspect of the soul that communes with God. There is no 'universal life energy' – or spirit as they would call it – animating the body. Any energy used as part of the body's operational functioning (such as the electricity in our nervous systems) is material in nature, and not spiritual.

The spirit was once considered to be the mental part of humanity. But that is overly simplistic – the mental aspect covers all brain functions, but not all are spiritual.

In some psychological models,[10] the human spirit is considered to be the mental functions of awareness, insight, understanding, judgement, and other reasoning powers. It is distinguished from the separate component of psyche, which comprises the qualities of emotion, passion, creativity, and personality. This is how the secularist tries to differentiate soul and spirit.

Some scholars view the human spirit merely as a social construct, representing the qualities of purpose and meaning which transcend the individual human being.[11] But the human spirit is not just a social construct. It is real.

And what about love? Is 'love' just another word for the 'spirit'? That's a tough one because it's hard to define exactly what love is. However, the love of God, the love of God-like attributes and behaviors, the love of communing with God, and the love of other creatures in the 'image of God', ARE qualities of the human spirit. Agape love is, by definition, spiritual in essence. Of course, the expression of love can be purely physical. But a deeper love is spiritual. In fact, in reality, love is the harmonious intermingling of two or more spirits. More on that in a later chapter.

THE FUNCTIONS

The word 'soul' can refer to both the immaterial and material aspects of humanity. Unlike human beings having a spirit, human beings are souls. In its most basic sense, the word 'soul' means 'life.' However, beyond this essential meaning, the Bible speaks of the soul in many contexts (doorway to sin, center of spiritual and emotional experience, etc.).[12] Whenever the word 'soul' is used, it can refer to the whole person, whether alive or in the afterlife.

The 'soul' is the energetic aspect of all living organisms – the life force or vitality of the organism.[13] In the human being, the 'soul' also contains the mind (intellect), emotions, and will – ways in which we contact all the things of the psychological realm. The human soul is 1) everlasting, 2) involved with thinking/intellect and

17

perceptions, and 3) the seat of self-consciousness. Altogether, it comprises who you are.[14]

The 'spirit', on the other hand, consists of the spiritual principle that exists within the soul, and it only resides in human beings.[15] It is our innermost part with which we contact God, and substantiate all the things of the spiritual realm. It is that which is of greatest value to a person – that by which he/she is most fully in God's 'image'.

The soul is how you relate to others and how you relate to yourself. The spirit is how you relate to God.[16] The soul gives a person the capacity for self-consciousness, but the spirit gives him/her the capacity for God-consciousness. The soul and spirit are our eternal true person, temporarily housed in a non-eternal body shell.

Although the spirit can be thought of as a fully integrated subfunction of the soul, there is not a physical duality of the soul/spirit. It is one unified whole.[17] The same is true for the 'wholeness' of the human being. There is not a triality of body/soul/spirit. It is a holistic integrated whole.

THE BATTLE BETWEEN SPIRITS

The spirit of a human being is the place where the Holy Spirit enters and tries to make the human spirit as God-like as possible. However, Satan can also enter through the spirit, with the intention of infiltrating the soul and controlling the emotions, by trying to make the soul succumb to sin and self-centeredness (through the affections). Satan knows that his victim is a creature of emotions, and it matters not if the emotions are stirred to sentimentalism or even to tears, just so long as the human's spirit does not come into harmony with the Holy Spirit.

The soul is the seat of the passions, the feelings, and the desires of the human being – the affections, right or wrong (love and hate, respect and lust). Satan's goal is to bend these towards his will by causing the person to worship only figments of their imagination (gods) created in the mentality of their soul, and not the one true God. Worshipping created gods is nothing but idolatry.

The soul is not directed toward God-centeredness until after the person's spirit has become regenerated by the Holy Spirit. A person's desires and affections are turned toward God when he realizes his sinful condition and God's grace in salvation. When the Holy Spirit illuminates the spirit of a person with divine light and life, that person begins to yield his/her affections and faculties to God.

In the words of the Blessed Virgin Mary, *"My soul glorifies the Lord, and my spirit rejoices in God my Savior."*[18] She could not praise the Lord in her soul until she had recognized God as her Savior in her spirit. Mary magnified the Lord in her soul, but she first enjoyed and experienced Him in her spirit.

We can never express God starting from our soul alone. We can try to mimic Him by trying our best to be good and holy, but even this always falls short of truly expressing God. This is because the true expression of God (magnifying the Lord) must come from our spirit, with God as its source and with our soul as its channel.

DESIGN AND CREATION

The human being occupies a unique place in creation: (1) it is 'in the image of God'; (2) by its own nature, it unites the spiritual and material worlds; (3) it is created as a trinity of male, female, and mutual interaction thereof; (4) God established it in His friendship.[19] ('it' being synonymous with 'he or she', which are human pronouns for gender)

Many people try to equate the 'image of God' to human abilities like abstract reasoning, having a conscience, or possessing an 'inner sense'. But being in 'the image of God' is a holistic trait – it's not possible to isolate any one attribute, or group of attributes – and it's not restricted to one sex; it is triune in nature – male, female, and the love of mutual interaction. Being most in 'the image of God' is the total bonding of two individuals. Indeed, our true expression of God comes from our 'spirit'.

The human being was designed by God to be bipartite in nature, with a male and female sex. But it was given an intelligence greater than any other creature – capable of advanced reasoning, and with the capacity to receive symbolic consciousness, sentience, and spirituality. This didn't happen by pure evolutionary chance. The communicable interaction of these abilities between the sexes renders them effectively tripartite in nature; a likeness with the Divine.[20]

It took almost all of the 5 trillion days of the universe unfolding after the Big Bang, to fabricate the first two individuals per the divine design.[21] But the design was so good that, even given the ills, misfortunes, harms, and injuries encountered in day-to-day living like any animal creature, it would be inevitable (perhaps with a little divine help along the way) that the creatures would adapt to all changing conditions, child-bearing would be prolific, and human beings would eventually exist all over the surface of the Earth.[22]

Every integrated soul and spirit, for all human beings, has been created by God outside of our space and time, and infused into living organic matter at conception – it is not 'produced' by the parents. The soul and non-activated spirit of all pure-blood descendants of pre-Adamites are similar.[23] For all lower order sexual cellular life forms, the soul is predesigned according to its intended kind and infused into the living organic matter at conception.[24]

Although the design of each soul is slightly different, it follows an evolutionary pattern that was determined by God at the beginning in His initial design concept.[25] It is driven by changeability due to historical 'adaptability' factors. Therefore, an evolutionary factor exists, and it may be thought that the soul is evolvable. However, the design of each spirit is uniquely tailored for each individual using criteria known only to God, and is not driven by changeability due to historical 'adaptability' factors. Therefore, the evolutionary factor is negligible – the spirit is not evolvable.

Furthermore, the soul and spirit (which includes all the intangible immaterial aspects of a person's makeup) of a human being are immortal: They do not perish when they separate from the body at death – they exist beyond the physical lifespan of the body – they are eternal – and they will be reunited with the body at the final Resurrection.[26]

NOTES

---

1 Biblical references to the human spirit can be found in Psalm 34:18, 142:3, 143:4,7; Isaiah 57:15, 66:2; Proverbs 15:13, 16:19, 17:22, 18:14; and Job 7:11, 17:1.

2 Life forms at a lower level of complexity than plants, fungi, and animals – the protists, bacteria, and archaea – have a proto-soul at the most fundamental level.

3. However, because of the 'Fall', the God-given soul and spirit are degraded in fidelity from what they were when originally given to Adam and Eve in the Garden of Eden.

4. The soul is accessed through the bodily senses, the rudimentary emotions (drives and instincts), and the mind. The spirit is accessed from the mind through the soul.

5. Human nature can also be considered as 'conscious spiritual existence'.

6. S. Warber, R. Bruyere, K. Weintrub, P. Dieppe, "Consideration of the Perspectives of Healing Practitioners on Research into Energy Healing", *Global Advances in Health and Medicine*, Vol. 4 Supplement, Nov 2015.

7. It is also worth noting that because there is no credible scientific substantiation for this energy, or the practices related to it, practitioners are not regulated and no professional standards are enforced.

8. Susan Brinkmann, "What you should know about Energy Medicine", *Living His Life Abundantly/Women of Grace*, February 15, 2023, Refer to: http://www.womenofgrace.com

9. The Holy See, "Jesus Christ – the Bearer of the Water of Life: A Christian Reflection on the 'New Age' "; *Pontifical Council for Culture – Pontifical Council for Interreligious Dialogue*; http://www.vatican.va

10. Daniel A. Helminiak, "Spirituality as an Explanatory and Normative Science", *Heythrop Journal* ,Vol. 52, Issue 4, 2011.

11. John Teske, "The Haunting of the Human Spirit", *Zygon*, Vol. 34 Issue 2, 2004.

12. Job 30:25; Psalm 43:5; Jeremiah 13:17; Luke 12:26

13. In the Bible, the term 'soul' often refers to human life in general, or to the entire human person – simply a more generalized definition applicable to humanity (especially to people saved into the Christian faith).

14. In the field of Psychology, the soul is considered as the seat of 1) the life-force, 2) intellect and rationality (comprised of memory, vocabulary/ideas, norms and standards, information indexing/filing, conscience, emotions, volition/will, and deductive reasoning), and 3) self-consciousness.

15. The unity of the soul and spirit together is sometimes called the 'spiritual soul'.

16. The soul is that which enables a person to function on the earthly plane – the spirit is that which enables a person to function on the divine plane, and walk with God in light and in truth (Reference: John 4:23-24).

17. From the analogous computer system viewpoint, you cannot identify specific lines of code for only the soul and for only the spirit. The coding is integrated – only some of the functionality is separately distinguishable.

18. Luke 1:46-47, (known as 'Mary's Song')

19. Catechism of the Catholic Church #343 (paraphrased)

20. The dual nature of the human creature, with its male and female sexes, and with an intrinsic emotional, spiritual, and physical bond between them (a communications channel of love and interaction), comprised a tripartite creation that was 'in the image' of the true triune God – two distinct 'persons', where the interaction is a fusion at such a high level of functionality, sentience, and love, that the interaction itself constitutes a 'person', the third person of a human trinity (a new creation of life, a newborn physical baby, being the most recognizable expression of the interaction).

The Father, Son, and Holy Spirit at the Divine level (The Holy Trinity), and the male, female, and interactive union (marriage/family) at the human physical level (the anthropomorphic trinity), are analogous.

21. The estimate of 5 trillion days is calculated as: $(13.798 \times 10^9 - 7.5 \times 10^3) \times 365.25 = 5{,}039{,}716{,}760{,}625$ days.

22. fulfilling the blessed command of God in Genesis 1:28

23. All homo-sapiens born before the appearance of Adam and Eve have a primitive internal soul and spirit, but the spirit has not been activated. All human beings born in the lineage of Adam and Eve have a more advanced soul, and a spirit that has been activated by God. In addition, all human beings born in the lineage of Seth, have an awakened spirit, capable of being filled by the Holy Spirit or by the spirit of the devil. Because of the 'original sin' by Adam and Eve, a 'veil' now exists over the human spirit – a curtain that hinders the infusion of the Holy Spirit, and allows for the devil Satan to gain entrance and even to gain strength.

24. Some atheists and evolutionists believe that the soul is a property emerging naturally from the complex organization of matter in the brain.

25. Although the design of each soul is slightly different, the design of each generation of soul, on the average, is also different – implying an evolutionary aspect to the design. If the average design of each generation was unchanged, then there would be no evolutionary factor.

26. The doctrine of the resurrection was generally accepted by the Jewish people and the Pharisees, but it was rejected by the Sadducees. Christ taught the doctrine of the resurrection when He said that the children of the resurrection will be equal to the angels. Refer to Luke 20:34-36. Our own risen bodies, reunited with our own souls and spirits, will share their rewards or punishments for all eternity. Also see: 1 Corinthians 15:20-23.

3 – THE VEILING OF THE SPIRIT

The word 'spirit' when used in the Bible has several meanings. Whenever the word is capitalized, it refers to the name of the third Person of the Trinity, the Holy Spirit of God. When the word is not capitalized, it can refer to the living spirit of a human being.[1]

Human beings have a spirit, but we are not spirits. However, in the Bible, only believers are said to be spiritually alive,[2] while unbelievers are spiritually dead.[3] The spirit is the element in humanity which gives us the ability to have an intimate relationship with God. When the word 'spirit' is used, it refers to the immaterial part of humanity that 'connects' with God, who Himself is pure spirit.[4]

The fact that the human spirit is intimately connected with the body is illustrated in the Old Testament, in Numbers 16:22, when Moses and Aaron call out, *'God of the **spirits** of all **flesh**'*.

The function of the spirit is a little less obvious than that of the body. While the function of the soul is to manifest God (through the intellect, emotions, and will), the function of the spirit is to contact and receive God (a spiritual task). Once we receive God into our spirit by believing in Him (in all three manifestations – Father, Son, and Holy Spirit),[5] we can live our human lives in continuous loving relationship with Almighty God by using our spirit.

The human spirit is what searches for universal, objective, spiritual truths involving self, life, and reality. The moral qualities of love, compassion, faith, hope, justice, and mercy, along with a certain measure of rationality, truthfulness, wisdom, and holiness, reside in the spirit. It is the immaterial facet of humanity that 'connects' with the one true God; the part with which we contact God and relate/interact with things in the divine realm. It enables the human to have a God-consciousness and function on the God-plane of existence. It is in the spirit of a person where the sphere of God-consciousness resides.

INFUSION OF THE HOLY SPIRIT

The human spirit can be enlightened by the Holy Spirit to be able to comprehend spiritual truths – truths like we need a Savior because of our sinful, fallen nature – and that the Savior has been revealed to us by the Father, through the Holy Spirit, as Jesus the Christ.

The [Holy] Spirit Himself gives witness with our spirit that we are children of God – Romans 8:16.[6]

God created human beings with the ability to experience theosis (the appreciation of the indwelling of the Holy Spirit within oneself) through an ongoing process of renewal or regeneration. Through this process, we are made alive, full, and complete – and we become a reflection of Him. Theosis is the transformation that takes place within the believer, a process that grows in time, by degrees, throughout our lives. As a result, there comes to the person a profound sense of unity with God.[7]

THE OPAQUE CURTAIN

Even though a person can be baptized, confirmed, or 'born-again', he/she can still be in bondage to sin (darkness or evil). That is because he/she has partially closed the portal to the spirit (like pulling down a window shade).

In reality, the portal is like a window that is always completely covered by a curtain or shade. This is called the 'veil' of the spirit. When the veil is totally opaque (closed or lowered), no external spiritual influence can enter. When the veil is totally transparent (open or raised), spiritual influence can enter. But, in addition to the Holy Spirit, demonic spirits can also enter, and then torment the person through their soul (mental illness, insanity) and/or through their body (infirmities).

The degree to which the spirit is veiled (the amount that the portal is transparent or opaque – open or closed – lowered or raised) is a continuous variable. It's as if the transparency of the veil, which completely covers the window, is controlled by the human will (from totally transparent – fully open – fully raised, to totally opaque – fully closed – fully lowered). If the veil has been opened and then closed, God cannot re-enter to bring healing and deliverance from satanic influence.

However, when we open again the veil and accept Jesus Christ as our Lord and Savior, our spirits become brand new. The darkness is washed away and we become a completely new person – born of God, and made alive with God.

Although our spirit is reborn when we open the veil and allow God to enter, our soul is not reborn. It must be washed clean by the renewing of our intellect, emotions, and will.[8] The seat of concupiscence is in the soul.[9] Therefore, the path to holiness is twofold: 1) Continually making sure that the veil of your spirit is open, and that the spirit is filled with the Holy Spirit (thereby keeping out the devil), and 2) Regularly cleansing the soul by renewing your intellect, emotions, and will through prayer, piety, and reading and meditating on the Word of God.[10]

THE TRANSPARENT CURTAIN

Because the human being embodies a 'spirit' that is divinely connected to the heavenly realm across all time and space, he/she is prearranged for a supernatural end – his/her soul can be gratuitously raised beyond all earthly worthiness, merit, and deserving – and forever become harmoniously in communion with God in Heaven.

Of all living creatures, only the human being is able to know and love his Creator. He is the only creature on earth that God has willed to be capable of sharing in the divine – and he alone is called to praise, by knowledge and through love and deed, in God's own existence. It was for this end that he was created, and this is the fundamental reason for his dignity.[11]

NOTES

1. 'spirit' with a small 's' can also refer to a demon, devil, or life-force – or emotions such as disposition, temperament, feeling, courage, or mettle.

2. Reference: 1 Corinthians 2:11; Hebrews 4:12; James 2:26

3. Reference: Ephesians 2:1-5; Colossians 2:13

4. John 4:24

5. Of course, this only applies to people born after the death and resurrection of Jesus Christ and the coming of the Holy Spirit. Prior to that, only belief in the one true Almighty God (later to be called the God of Abraham) could result in receiving God into the spirit (although there could be some leeway for good people outside of the Abrahamic bloodline – a thorny theological issue).

In modern times, there are many people who believe in a unitarian God and not a trinitarian God (Jews, Muslims, Universalists). They too, can have a loving relationship with God, but it is a theological mystery as to exactly how close the loving relationship is from the standpoint of God.

6. Satan cannot challenge our position as 'children of God', but he can contest our performance as 'children of God' – the essence of 'Spiritual Warfare'. The battleground is in our souls.

7. Full realization of our oneness with God comes only after death. This is called divinization.

8. Refer to Romans 12:12.

9. The continuous inclination toward sin and evil in the fallen human being is called 'concupiscence'.

10. Open the Bible, and open-up to the Lord – incline your heart to Him. Then read a few Bible verses and turn them into short, spontaneous prayers to the Lord – thanking Him, praising, or petitioning Him as you feel led. In this way, you can enter into fellowship with Him in your spirit.

11. Catechism of the Catholic Church #356 (paraphrased)

4 – WHERE THE SPIRIT RESIDES

Each cell in a living organism is like a microcomputer, complete with input/output interface, logic unit (microprocessor), control unit, memory, data buses, power supply, and software (see Appendix C for a more complete analogy). A nerve cell has a more powerful logic unit,[1] and a nerve cell in the brain has the most powerful logic unit for the organism.[2]

All the cells are connected together in a communications network – like the cellular network or Internet – forming a vast distributed information processing system.[3] The logical processing is distributed throughout the many cells in the network – in the tissues, organs, and organ systems – resulting in a massively parallel processing system, that can process large amounts of data near simultaneously (to perform many functions at the same time).

The cell is nature's version of a technology-based system-of-systems at the micro-level. If you go inside, it's a complex set of interconnected machinery. The fundamental machines that make up the cell are molecules, and they're subject to the same chemical and physical laws as they would be outside the cell.[4]

The complete organism is nature's version of a technology-based system-of-systems at the macro-level.[5] There is a transfer of data and information at all interior levels in order to produce the desired effect at each level. It is a hierarchically nested, embedded and filtered, multiple system-of-systems (each system containing an associated control program – which may be hard or soft coded), where the individual systems, subsystems, and sub-subsystems (down to what we like to think of as the 'unit' level – the cell) – and groups of nested systems (a system-of-systems slice) – bi-directionally communicate with each other over network paths, are learnable (sometimes called evolvable), adaptive, self-adjusting, fault tolerant, and semi-autonomous – and where the system, subsystem, or 'unit', is self-replicating.

That's a lot of wordsmithing, but it's just a description of a modern large-scale technological enterprise (like the air traffic control system or electrical power grid), but without the self-replicating feature (which is unique to biology).

Spread throughout the memory of all the networked cells, and launched/executed by processors within the cells (for different functions in different cells to varying degrees), is the executable program code of the Operating System – a distributed Operating System – that manages groups of distinct cells and makes them appear to be a single cell.[6] Distributed logic processing is carried out in more than one cell (when cells in a group work in cooperation, they form a distributed system). Thus, each cell contains a little piece of the overall Operating System. This is where the 'soul' of the organism resides.

Concentrated in the nerve cells of the brain and the nervous system (especially near the heart), and launched/executed by processors within these cells, is the executable code of the Application Program. The overall program is distributed across the applicable cells – each nerve cell containing a little piece of the overall Application Program. This is where the 'spirit' of the human being resides.[7]

Thus, the Operating System and the Application Program are intimately and harmoniously related – just exactly as is the soul and the spirit in a human being.

NOTES

1. 'power' meaning logical operations per second, or throughput

2. For a good highly technical reference, see: Gerd HG Moe-Behrens, "The Biological Microprocessor, or How to Build a Computer with Biological Parts"; *Computational and Structural Biotechnology Journal*, Vol. 7, Issue: 8, April 2013.

3. An information system utilizes information, and the complementary networks of hardware and software, to collect, filter, process, create, and distribute data. The information system has a definitive boundary, users, processors, stores, inputs, outputs, and communication networks. The information system is intended to support operations, management, and decision making within a larger process.

4. The living and the non-living differ in the degree of communication between scales. In living systems, information passes back and forth between every level, from sub-cellular proteins, through organelles (the units within a cell), to tissues, and organs. However, at the molecular scale, there is no difference between living and non-living.

5. More precisely, astronomical phenomena are nature's version of a technology-based system-of-systems at the macro-level. An organism could be considered to be at mid-level. But that distinction is irrelevant for this illustration. Of course, one could go further up above macro to the grand-scale gravitational and relativistic aspects of astrophysical phenomena. Likewise, one could go further down below micro to the probabilistic aspects of atoms, molecules, and sub-atomic particles.

6. The development of networked computers that could be linked and communicate with each other, providing each other with data and information, gave rise to distributed computing.

7. The Operating System provides an interface between an application program and the hardware (especially for input/output and memory allocation). It manages the overall hardware and software resources, and provides common services for the application program. The application program can interact with the hardware only by obeying

rules and procedures programmed into the Operating System. The application code makes frequent system calls to the Operating System, or is interrupted by it, to provide information services.

5 – THE SPIRIT IN THE CREATION STORY

"How exactly did this all occur?" you might ask.

Well, sometime around 4.6 billion years ago, God intervened in the ongoing physical evolutionary process of the universe in order to 'help' form the planet Earth (the concept and blueprint for which He had designed before the beginning of time).[1] He then 'helped along' the first formation of non-living matter into living matter about 3.8 billion years ago,[2] and infused a rudimentary soul into cellular life about 1.2 billion years ago,[3] when sexual reproduction first appeared. Over time, as the biodiversity of Earth burgeoned, the complexity of the soul program changed accordingly – ranging from the most primitive to the very complex. The simpler the life form, the more elementary the soul, and vice versa.[4]

It should come as no surprise, then, that Adam and Eve were not the very first human-like beings on Earth.[5] Instead, they should be thought of as the first humanoid creatures that were chosen by God to be worthy of originating a pathfinder lineage (a group of individuals related by descent from a common ancestor), and therefore given the gift of certain attributes that would enable them to be more in the 'image of God' than the other co-existing creatures at the time (although not a 100% perfect image because of the finite limitations of the organic human vessel containing the soul and spirit, when existing in a non-spirit realm – in other words, the physical limitations of an earthly body).[6]

Because God is pure infinite spirit, to be 'in the image of God' implies that a spirit is infused into the human-like being. And Adam and Eve were the first human-like beings to be given the gift of an advanced soul with heightened awareness, reasoning, will, symbolic consciousness,[7] and sentience [8]– and a divine ethereal spirit activated with God-consciousness. All the other human-like beings at the time have a less advanced soul and a non-activated spirit. Thus, Adam and Eve were the first beings containing an advanced soul <u>and</u> an activated spirit – the first true human beings.[9]

By the gift of an advanced soul and an activated spirit, God gave Adam and Eve the potential to be as much like God as it is possible for a physical created being to be.[10] Of course, there are some incommunicable attributes of God, such as unchangeableness, timelessness, omniscience, omnipresence, and omnipotence. None of these characteristics could be given to Adam and Eve, even in their unfallen state. They were still subject to their physical material limits as created beings.

CHILDREN OF GOD

The greatest present bestowed by God on humanity, as the result of receiving a divinely created activated spirit, is the gift of **sanctifying grace** – which makes them 'children of God', and gives them the right to have access to heaven. Sanctifying grace is a supernatural gift which is a sharing in the nature of God Himself, and which raises human beings to the supernatural order, conferring on them powers entirely above those fitting their primal ungifted nature.[11]

But Adam and Eve were not given this grace. In their 'unfallen' state, it was not necessary – they were already sanctified. Unlike the animals and other primitive humanoids, Adam and Eve alone were endowed with a higher order soul and a special ethereal spirit activated for God-like consciousness. Being now in the 'likeness of God' (in His image), they were blessed with an intellect and a will. They had the capacity to rise above their instincts, and participate in the divine spiritual life.

In preparation for their stewardship over creation, God first gave Adam and Eve mastery over themselves. They were created in a state of 'original justice' – all of their doings (desires, pleasures, aims, and drives) were guided by goodness and reason of heart. He offered them His own heart and His fellowship as the First Covenant.[12] As part of that original covenant of love, God gave Adam and Eve everything that lived – that had the breath of life – for them to utilize and manage for His glory. Humanity was originally meant to cooperate with God in the continued/ongoing work of creation.[13]

But, as we all know, much of this was lost at the 'Fall', when they sinned against God – and did the one thing they were commanded not to do. They lost their sanctification.

The Blessing of Seth

The blessing of the species of human beings begins with Seth, the third son of Adam and Eve. Seth is the first person after the 'Fall' to receive the divine gift of sanctifying grace – not the full measure, but a spark. At a pivotable moment in history, the 'Word of God' spoke directly to Seth, something like this:

Seth, My child, listen to Me now! You are blessed from on High – blessed above all the others. You are the favored son of Eve – the one who will father a new race of people – a race that will be My people, and I will be their God. You are the one who will replace Abel the Just, the first to be blessed. You are gifted in body, mind, and spirit – and your soul is pure. But prepare yourself! Another gift awaits you – the gift of sanctifying grace! The spark of divinity will enter your spirit as the seed of eternity – your spirit will become even more deeper than before. Listen up now! Know that this is a spark and not the entire flame. The final imprint of divinity, the flame of immortality, will come at a later time as a Pentecostal gift to your descendants. I will prepare them for it and see to it Myself.[14] Seth, favored child of God, are you prepared and willing to receive this gift? [15]

Seth accepts the offer and receives the spark of divinity – apotheosis – and is moved one step closer to divinization – theopoiesis – by divine grace through union with the Holy Spirit. He doesn't receive the full measure of sanctifying grace, just a spark – a sample. But his children are blessed and also receive the spark.[16]

After the death and resurrection of Jesus Christ, at the time of Pentecost, the Holy Spirit is poured out on the apostles,[17] and the full gift of sanctifying grace is brought with Him. All people at that time (including Jews, Samaritans, pagans, and atheists) become eligible to receive the Holy Spirit's gift of sanctifying grace, if they sincerely put their faith in Jesus Christ as their personal savior (they become Christianized).[18] Their spirit is activated, and the gift is available to all. Will and faith are all that is required.

TALKING TO GOD THROUGH PRAYER

The key mechanism by which we communicate with God through our spirit is by prayer. It is the directing of one's affections, the lifting up of one's soul – one's heart and mind – to God. It is a devout and friendly talk with Him. It has been said that prayer is the tranquility of the mind when illuminated from above.[19]

Prayer has existed since the time of Adam and Eve – which makes perfect sense since Adam and Eve were the first human creatures to have a God-given activated spirit. During the first 200 days after expulsion from the Garden of Eden, through frequent intervention by the Angel of the Word, Adam and Eve learned how to pray.[20] They prayed often, with humility and devotion, for the rest of their lives – and taught their children, and their children's children, how to pray.

Forms of Prayer

Basically, there are two forms of prayer: the prayer of worship, and the prayer of petition. Prayers of worship are usually thanks for blessings,[21] gratitude for God's goodness and mercy,[22] or praise of God for creation.[23] Adam and Eve prayed all these forms with the right intention, with honor to God.

Prayers of petition can be for many different things, as each person has different needs and desires. Adam and Eve prayed especially for the strength to lead a virtuous life.[24] And Eve, in particular, prayed for wisdom (occasioned by her sin in the Garden),[25] and for children (occasioned by the death of Abel the Just).[26]

Mental prayer is the wordless raising up of the heart and mind to God.[27] Meditation and contemplation are the most common types of mental prayer. Meditation can be described as prayer by reasoning, while contemplation, the highest form of mental prayer, is a song of the heart – a harmony of the will. In this state, the mind mentally gazes upon God with a deep, fervent love.

It usually requires a very committed and devout person to reach this state of rapture in prayer. But the ability to engage in this deep type of prayer is sometimes given by God, as a special free gift, to help one get rid of sinful inclinations. In this case, it is called 'infused contemplation'. Adam and Eve were given this special gift to ease the burden of their instantaneous transition from a state of innocence to a state of sinfulness, as a result of their actions in the Garden of Eden.

The grace of God is great.

NOTES

---

1. By 'help', the implication is that supernatural forces rather than natural forces are at play here – and that an intelligence lies behind the workings of the supernatural forces, so as to guide the unfolding of events driven by those forces. It is our custom to call that intelligence divine, and the essence of divinity as 'God'.

The concepts of 'control' and 'design' are prominent in our understanding of the attributes of 'God'. When we control or design a process, we are helping to steer its progressing state, so that the downstream outcome will be as desired. That model of reality is what is at work here. God has been, and still is (maybe now to a slightly lesser degree) controlling and designing (by the use of design changes or tweaks [some say fine-tuning or upgrading], made after the initial design) the grand process of a time-based reality, that manifests to us as an evolutionary unfolding of physical events – the evolution of the universe and the earth.

The all-intelligent 'God' does this in order to keep the process efficiently moving, or progressing, toward His desired final state. Note that this pattern is ongoing and all-encompassing. Creation of the planet earth, suitable for the emergence and development of 'life' did not end the process. Furthermore, there is an infinite number of hierarchical processes going on at the same time – and they are related, interconnected, and interdependent. That is the underlying framework when it is said that God intervened in the ongoing physical evolutionary process of the universe in order to 'help' form the planet Earth.

2. The scientific term is abiogenesis.

3. The soul can be imagined as an information-based program, or interactive database, that regulates and drives the life processes of a living organism.

4. There may have been many other interventions by God prior to the creation of the Earth, during its formative history, during the development of life, and during the evolution of intelligent life. The appearance of major disruptive events in the astronomical and geological record may hint at divine interventions. There are many

examples of this. In fact, from the probability standpoint, it's almost as if it could be utterly impossible for everything that has happened to have happened by pure chance.

In fact, this is a formal argument for the existence of God, called the 'Fine Tuning Argument'. This argument claims that the laws of nature, the constants of physics, and the initial conditions of the universe are finely tuned for conscious life. Often cited as evidence are several dozen "cosmic constants" whose parameters are such that if they were altered even slightly, conscious life would be impossible. Three major examples are: (1) If the strong nuclear force (the force that binds protons and neutrons in an atom) had been either stronger or weaker by five percent, life would be impossible; (2) If neutrons were not roughly 1.001 times the mass of protons, all protons would have decayed into neutrons, or vice versa, and life would be impossible; (3) If gravity had been stronger or weaker by one part in 1040, life-sustaining stars, including the sun, could not exist; thus life would most likely be impossible. While each of the representative examples may not be fully accurate, it is argued that the significant number of them, coupled with their independence from one other, provides evidence of their being intentionally established with conscious life in mind – in other words, designed. Furthermore, the design may have been tweaked or upgraded, over time, as deemed fit by the designer.

God often uses natural forces to steer (or guide) the natural unguided evolutionary processes in order to obtain the desired corrective effect. The practice of tweaking the design after its instantiation (remember, the ongoing evolutionary process was itself designed by God at the very beginning), by slightly altering the appropriate parameters, is a common practice in conventional design engineering).

5. These primitive beings with a less advanced soul, and a God-infused but un-activated spirit, are sometimes called 'pre-Adamites'.

6. Living some 7500 years ago in the ancient Near East, Adam and Eve represent iconic 'avatars' for the rest of humanity. By this time, proto-humans had already dispersed throughout most of the earth.

God then revealed himself with special favor and intention to a pair of highly developed creatures we know as Adam and Eve – real people whom God selected as 'test subjects' for His creative embodiment of a creature that would have the ability to comprehend the divine reality – and one-day, rejoin with the Holy Family in Heaven.

7. Heightened awareness, reasoning, will, and symbolic consciousness – these are traits that enable an individual to perceive, reason, and respond to selected features of the environment, and to rationally interact with other beings – note that it is likely that primitive awareness and elemental consciousness were given to some of the higher order animals and hominins long ago.

8. Sentience is the capacity to feel, empathize, and relate to the environment, and with other beings in a reasoned and shared manner – sometimes also called phenomenal consciousness, subjective consciousness, secondary consciousness, or intentionality – note that this may include the capacity to think about, and therefore conceptualize, one's own thoughts – to be self-aware and self-conscious.

9. The term 'human being' is arbitrarily associated with creatures of the homo-sapiens species that have received an advanced soul and ethereal spirit by direct gift from God, and not by slow evolutionary development. A purely scientific definition would equate human beings with homo-sapiens (the only non-extinct species in the genus Homo).

Over time, a more sophisticated soul would slowly evolve in all human-like creatures. But at the time of Adam and Eve, only that couple possessed an advanced soul and an activated spirit 'in the image of God' (known as spiritual vigor). All the other creatures had a lower-level soul and a non-activated spirit. Identifying Adam and Eve as the first true human beings is just a semantic classification. It is not a scientific or sociological determination.

An interesting theory is that over time, in different places around the world and in different cultures, additional Adam and Eve type creatures were selected by God and given an advanced soul and an activated spirit in varying stages of fidelity. This could help explain the mysticism of some Far Eastern and Indian religions.

10. Of course, this potential was temporarily reduced by 'the Fall' of Adam and Eve in the Garden of Eden. The reduction is significant, but we don't know exactly how much. If we are 'saved' by the loving acceptance of Jesus Christ as our personal savior and redeemer, then that initial potential will be restored when we rejoin the Holy Family in the divine realm of Heaven.

11. The loss of sanctifying grace marked the beginning of the conflict between man's lower drives and his sense of reason, of which Saint Paul says, *"The flesh lusts against the spirit, and the spirit against the flesh . . ."* (Galations 5:17).

12. Genesis 1:28-29 is generally considered to be the first covenant between God and humanity – where the human being (Adam and Eve in this story) is given dominion over all living things and allowed to be fruitful and multiply – in exchange for obedience and praise of God.

13. in the Latin, Homo Pontifex – the Natural Priest – the builder of bridges – one who has two dimensions – who creates with God and who reflects the majesty of creation back to God

14. The ministry of Jesus Christ on earth.

15. Seth willfully makes a decision – in a manner similar to the Blessed Virgin Mary, who willfully made a decision when proffered by the angel Gabriel (Luke 1:26-38). Probably, the two greatest decisions in all of history.

16. Eve tells Enosh, the firstborn son of Seth to listen to his counsel. Ancient records reveal her saying, "My dear Enosh, listen to me now. You must always carefully listen to the counsel of Seth. And you must tell all of the other brothers and sisters, sons and daughters, to also listen to his counsel. Listen to him not only as a father, but also as a mentor. For he now has the spark of divinity within him."

17. Acts 2:1-21

18. Christian baptism activates sanctifying grace, but a person only receives the full measure of sanctifying grace if he/she sincerely puts his/her faith in Jesus Christ as his/her personal savior.

19. Companions of Saint Anthony, *Companion Prayers: A Guide to Prayer* [Ellicott City, MD: Franciscan Voice, 2013].

20. The Angel of the Word – the Word of God – the Logos – the Second Person of the Holy Trinity – Refer to: Edward N. Brown, *The Passion of Eve: Remembering the Beginning* [Chicago: Crystal Sea Press, 2019].

21. Psalms 65:2-14

22. Psalms 34:5-23

23. Psalms 8:4-10; 19:2-7; 33:6-15; Job 26:7-14

24. Psalms 5:9

25. Wisdom 9:1-12

26. 1 Samuel 1:9-11 (Hannah's Prayer)

27. Prayers may be said vocally – privately or publicly – or one may pray mentally. God listens to all prayers and answers them either by granting the petition requested, or by substituting something else that He knows is best for the person. Those who pray with all sincerity, ask God with the fullness of their spirit, to subordinate their own wills to His – because only God knows what one really needs in this earthly realm of existence.

6 – THE ESSENCE OF THE SPIRIT

Within the canopy of Divine Reality containing created beings, God determined that two polarities should exist – 'Good' and 'the deprivation of Good'. Why this is so is another great mystery because God Himself is the perfect essence of 'Good'. But it is the way of things. It is our reality.

Being the perfect essence of 'Good', God could not create 'Bad' (or 'evil'). Yet 'Bad' seems to exist. This conundrum has plagued philosophers for centuries. Because of our finite brains and limited intellectual ability, we cannot fully comprehend or understand this enigma. But some of our greatest theologians (including Saint Thomas Aquinas) have postulated it like this:[1] 'Bad' does not exist in a manner that we think it does. What we refer to as 'Bad' (or 'evil') is actually that which once was 'Good', but for some reason has been deprived of some of that 'Good' (a loose analogy is a sighted person who then goes near-blind). 'Good' can exist without 'Bad', but 'Bad' cannot exist without 'Good'. In other words, 'Bad' is the absence of 'Good', but only in the sense that 'Good' had to once be present for there to be an absence of it.

Now there is a continuum in the 'Good' parameter from '100% Good' to '0% Good' (which could be stated as '100% Bad'). But even at '0% Good' (the worst case), the truth is that the original '100% Good' had to have been lost.

The deprivation of 'Good' comes about by the awareness that there exists the freedom to choose self-centeredness. We think this is driven by pride and envy, but that is just our rationalization of it. Self-centeredness puts oneself above that of others, and above that of God. It puts self-interest above the interest of God and all of His creation. When this occurs, some amount of 'Good' is lost. As human beings, we comprehend this incremental loss of 'Good' as 'Bad' (or 'evil'). Total God-centeredness is '100% Good' and total self-centeredness is '0% Good' (or '100% Bad'). Exactly what behavior constitutes the percentage of 'Good' at every point along the continuum has been established by God within the framework of eternal divinity, and is known only to Him.

All created entities (beings) with the gift of consciousness (simply put, an intelligence sufficiently developed for conscious thought and reflection), have an innate awareness of self-centeredness and God-centeredness.

As a gift from God, the desire for 'Good' (or God-centeredness) has been hard-coded into the spirit of all conscious beings (for human beings, we also say it is written 'in the heart'). But just as the desire for 'Good' is written into the being's spirit, so also is the awareness that the freedom to move away from God-centeredness to self-centeredness ('Bad') exists in that same spirit.[2]

As the first chosen human beings made in God's image, Adam and Eve were beings high in the divine hierarchy – they possessed an awareness of total God-centeredness ('100% Good'). But they also possessed 'free-will' and the awareness that the freedom to choose self-centeredness existed. Of course, as we all know, when introduced into the overall celestial family in the Garden of Eden, there was a loss of 'Good' when they chose incorrectly. The rest is history.

THE 'ANGELIC FALL'

But first, a bit about the angels and their state of affairs:

The angel Lucifer actually sought to be on a higher footing than God – not outright rejection of God, but elevation of himself above God. His sin was the elevation of self-centeredness over God-centeredness (some would say egotism or vanity). In the angelic realm, this was the gravest of all transgressions. Since the existence of God could not be challenged, only the authority of God could be challenged.

Eventually there was a 'war' in the spirit realm – the outcome being the banishment of all challenging angels (the 'fallen angels') from Heaven, to which they previously had access.[3] The resulting consequences hugely affected all of reality, including our own corporeal reality (especially in the Garden of Eden).[4] The theology is very intricate and profound.[5]

The account of the 'Fall' of Adam and Eve in Genesis 3 is couched in such terms that it is impossible to see in it anything more than the acknowledgment of the existence of a 'personal' principle of evil – a 'person' who was jealous of the human race. The individualization of that principle of evil is Lucifer, or Satan (or the 'Devil'), an entity created as a good angel, but who later became the leader of all the bad angels who had become unfaithful, and lost the grace of God.[6] When the angels were created, God bestowed upon them great wisdom, power, holiness, and a supernatural grace by which they could gain eternal happiness in Heaven – they were given the opportunity to merit the rewards of Heaven by remaining faithful to God.

We do not know the exact nature of the test to which God put the angels (similar to the test given to Adam and Eve with the Tree of the Knowledge of Good and Evil),[7] but there was a 'situation' in which their faithfulness and resolve was tested. The angels who did not remain faithful to God were cast into hell (but with a passageway to the Earth), in what has been called 'the war in Heaven',[8] and condemned to eternal punishment. These bad angels are called 'devils' (often called 'evil spirits' by primitive humans). They were created by God as good beings, but by their own free-will and acts, they chose the way of evil, and thereby became 'fallen' angels. This is known as the 'angelic Fall'.

The 'angelic fall' preceded the formation of life on earth, and this is why different forms of 'loss of Good' (predation, parasitism, bloodsucking, etc.) existed on earth prior to the appearance of Adam and Eve. It may also explain why the Garden of Eden was necessary. And it is the root cause for 'original sin' and concupiscence that exist in the human spirit.

THE 'HUMAN FALL'

Satan was entrusted to honor Adam and Eve, so that they could develop to a state of high fellowship with God. But Satan was jealous of the human beings. He believed that they would become elevated over himself in the hierarchy of creatures, and thereby closer to God. He resented this because he was their senior in the Creation, and therefore thought himself to be superior. He knew there would be a 'situation' in which their faithfulness and resolve would be tested, similar to what occurred with the angels. So, he contrived to rig the test and assure that they would fail, thereby nudging them down the hierarchy of creatures lower than him, and condemning them also to eternal punishment.

However, God was not tricked by Satan's ploy. He could see through the facade of the satanic plan and would not allow for such an outcome.

And for that impertinence, Satan was forever banished from Heaven along with his followers, the 'fallen' angels. They still keep the great powers natural to a pure spirit (they can do things that seem like miracles to us), and although their passageway to Earth remains, they are not given the power to force the humans to sin. But alas, they retain the power to tempt them – to try and steer them into sin. It happened in the Garden of Eden (you know the story)[9] and it happens every day to every person on planet earth.

The spirits of Adam and Eve were veiled. It was almost as if a pulled-down translucent window shade (or a foggy curtain) was placed over their spirit. Their grasp of God and His presence had become blurred and less distinct.[10] And because their free-will action of eating the forbidden fruit from the Tree of the Knowledge of Good and Evil was the cause of the blurring, this act was the 'original sin'. Furthermore, this veiling of the spirit was now inheritable. All of their descendants would now be born with a veiled foggy spirit. But it was still a spirit in 'the image of God' – understanding that the word 'image' itself connotes a certain amount of fogginess in the picture. They were still greater than the animals and the primitive humanoids whose spirit was not activated.

THE TENDENCY TO SIN

Although we have the behavioral gift of 'free-will' in our spirit, because of the fogginess in that spirit (the relative level of transparency of the veil), we have the tendency to sin – the innate tendency to want to disobey God, and travel along the 'way of darkness' rather than the 'way of light'. This is because of the 'original sin' at 'the Fall', and the consequent disorder known as concupiscence.[11]

Adam and Eve committed the very first human sin, the 'original sin'; the stain of which was then immersed into the activated spirit of every human being who has been born since then [12](except for two –the Blessed Virgin Mary in the Immaculate Conception, and our Lord Jesus Christ in the Hypostatic Union).

Furthermore, the continuous inclination toward sin and evil is called concupiscence. Baptism forgives 'original sin' and turns a person back towards God (he is forgiven).[13]

But the inclination toward sin and evil persists, and one must always continue to struggle against it,[14] and ask for forgiveness. Confession and reconciliation are services provided by the church that represent visible signs of invisible grace, that are instituted to help in our justification.[15]

REGENERATING THE SPIRIT

In the unfallen state, the human spirit was illuminated from Heaven, becoming the epicenter of God-consciousness. But when the human race fell in Adam and Eve, sin veiled the portal to the spirit, causing it to be difficult for the Holy Spirit to enter and bring a God-like consciousness.[16] It also became more difficult for the Holy Spirit to wash away the satanic spirits that still could enter. This condition remains in every unbaptized person (or in a baptized person who has willfully rejected the baptism, or refused to accept a renewal) until he has willfully accepted a new baptism – when the light and life-giving power of the Holy Spirit floods into the human spirit with the divine appreciation of a new life in Christ Jesus. The veil is 'lifted' – opened – made more transparent. But unfortunately, it will tend to fall again in time and require constant 'lifting'. The spirit is like the human being's private office, where the ongoing work of regeneration takes place.[17]

The human spirit requires the 'spark of baptism' or the 'bath of regeneration' before there is an understanding of the things of God. His spiritual nature must be awakened or renewed before there is a true conception of Godliness. Only one thing controls the veil over a person's spirit, and that is his/her own will (whether mature or naive, it matters not). When the will is surrendered, the veil is lifted and the Holy Spirit takes up His abode in the person's spirit. And when that occurs, he becomes alive again – a 'child of God'.[18]

Baptism followed by Confirmation followed by Communion [some say to be 'born again'] is the best way to obtain the standing of 'child of God' (and very importantly, to retain it).[19]

THE NATURE OF LOVE

What is love? Ask any person and you'll get many different answers. Some will say, "It's that warm fuzzy feeling that you get when you are attracted to someone." Others will say, "It's when you are physically intimate with someone who you like." In either case, it's a physical reaction – a physical sensation. And most people would agree.

But then there is the question, what is God? Or, what is the prime attribute of God? Most people will say, "God is love" – a succinct and encompassing definition. And most people would agree.

The answers to these two questions seem perfectly right and reasonable. But are they? If God is pure spirit, how could He feel physical sensation? Conversely, if love is a physical thing, how could it be associated with God, a purely spiritual entity?

The answer is straightforward, but it has escaped the grasp of most human beings for centuries.

Simply put, love is the harmonious interaction of two or more spirits.

Physical sensation can be a consequence, but it is not the essence of love. When a human spirit harmoniously interacts with God (or the spirit of God), then love is present.[20] When a human spirit harmoniously interacts with another human spirit, then love is present. It's been said that you know that you're in love if you sense that your spirits are linked in harmony. True words of wisdom.

In a similar manner, God loves humanity, His triumphant creation. His spirit harmoniously interacts with the spirits of many human beings. In the beginning, it was with a couple, a pair of creatures – Adam and Eve. Their spirits were activated, enabling them to interact with God and with each other. God loved them, they loved God, and they loved each other. They were given dominion over the earth, but were responsible for its stewardship through devoutness to God.[21]

Later in time, God's love was with a family, the family of Noah. Their spirits interacted and God loved them so much, that He saved them from the great deluge, to start a new lineage of God-fearing people. They were given life and a new world to settle, but they were to remain devoted to God. They were given dominion over the earth but were to be held accountable to God's commands.[22]

Later still, God's love was with a tribe, the extended family, slaves, and workers of Abraham. He loved them so much that He gave them the land of Canaan and promised descendants as numerous as the stars in the sky, in return for devoutness to God.[23]

Still later, God's love was with a nation – the nation of the Israelites – with the people under Moses, David, and Solomon. He loved them so much that He brought them out of bondage in Egypt, and established them as the supreme proprietors of Canaan. Their only charge was to love the one true God and keep His commandments.[24]

In succeeding years, there were breakdowns in the covenant – many people lost their faith and love for God – and suffering and tribulation occurred, as the love between God and His 'chosen' people was tested.[25] But the spiritual bond between God and His 'chosen' people remained – God's love did not falter.

The commandments of God gradually became the Law of the Hebrews, as the religious leaders constantly sought to stem the tide of disorder in the faith and the creeping influence of pagan worship, by creating new and more restrictive laws. But the laws became a hindrance in and of themselves – few people could keep the laws, and massive sacrifices for repentance became the commercialized norm. Eventually, there came the time when a sign was needed to reassure the people that the nation would not dissolve – so, a divine sign was given to Ahaz and Isaiah, as follows:

A virgin will be found with child, and she will bear a son and name him Immanuel. A descendant of Jesse, the spirit of the Lod will rest upon Him – a spirit of wisdom and understanding – of counsel, of strength, and of knowledge. He will become a signal to the nations – the Gentiles will seek Him out, and His kingdom will be glorious.[26]

With the miraculous birth of Jesus Christ, the prophetic sign became truth. In the beginning was the Word – the Word was made flesh – and the Word dwelt among us. He was filled with enduring love – love following upon love – a love meant for all. The Law was given through Moses, but enduring love came through Jesus Christ.[27] God's love was now with all the people of the earth. His spirit could interact with the spirits of most all humans, and harmonious interaction was up to the will of the individual.

With the coming of the Holy Spirit, the human spirits have become awakened – to more readily communicate and interact with God in a harmonious fashion – and to receive the gift of sanctifying grace. The love of God is great. All that is required to fully receive the love of God – His gift of salvation and eternal life – is the will of the person. But Satan will test that will.

NOTES

1. Thomas Aquinas, *The Summa Theologica of St. Thomas Aquinas* (London: Burns, Oates & Washbourne, 1912). Online at http://www.newadvent.org/summa.

2. The degree (or percentage) of God-centeredness or self-centeredness at any point (in time for corporeal beings), can be likened to journeying along a long divided bi-directional highway with multiple crossover gates (or doors), and with everlasting life and everlasting death as the two endpoints. Where you are on the highway, relative to the endpoints, represents the degree of God-centeredness or self-centeredness of the person.

3. Revelation 12:7-9

4. The temptation of Adam and Eve in the Garden of Eden presupposes the existence of bad spirits or demons, who were cast into hell from which they have no hope of redemption. This was the result of the 'angelic Fall' following the 'war in heaven'.

5. For a good synopsis of the story, see Ron Rhodes, "How Did Lucifer Fall and Become Satan?" 2018, *Christianity.com*. Accessed Nov. 2018 at https://www.christianity.com/theology/theological-faq/.

6. The term sometimes used for the aggregate of all the bad angels is 'The Satan' (with the definite article).

7. Genesis 2:15-17

8. The angelic war in heaven is aptly covered by Hugh Pope, "Angels", *The Catholic Encyclopedia*, Vol. 1 (New York: Robert Appleton Company, 1907), 14 Dec. 2017; accessed Nov. 2018 at http://www.newadvent.org/cathen/01476d.htm.

9. If you don't know the story, see Genesis 3.

10. In the Bible, it is said that *the eyes of both of them were opened*. Refer to Genesis 3:7.

11. Remember that the continuous inclination toward sin and evil in the fallen human being is called 'concupiscence'.

12. Pure-blood descendants of pre-Adamites (up until the time of Christ) do not have an activated spirit, and therefore, do not suffer from the effects of 'original sin'. They do not know that their sins are sins, and therefore, they will not be judged by God for their sinful actions. After the resurrection of Christ, all people born have an activated spirit.

13. The early European explorers, conquistadores, and missionaries were eager to baptize the natives, such that they could be 'saved'. Their spirit was activated but it needed to be filled with the Holy Spirit. There was genuine concern. Unfortunately, the initial attempts at evangelization were less than successful. The indigenous people were different than the pagans of Europe or the Near East, and required a different approach. This problem remained until intervention by the Blessed Virgin Mary in the apparition of 'Our Lady of Guadalupe', after which, in a very short period of time, nearly all of South and Central America converted to Christianity.

14. All human beings with an activated spirit are marred by the sin and evil they have committed. It is inherently in our nature, our inclination – we can't help it – it is marked by the concupiscence within rational choice and the inherited stain of 'original sin' (the mentally disabled, the intellectually immature, and even newborn babies are not exempt from this).

15. A sacrament is an outward sign instituted by Christ which produces interior grace. The act of Penance and Reconciliation (which includes contrition, confession, and penance) is a formal Sacrament of the Catholic church.

16. As an example, if an unbaptized (or unregenerate) person has a will to know certain scientific facts, then by his human spirit, he is enabled to investigate, think, and weigh evidence. If he concentrates and works hard, he may become a famous scientist or have great accomplishments. However, his spirit is limited to the things of this world. If he wants to know about the things of God, his unenlightened spirit is not up to the task.

17. *The (Holy) Spirit Himself gives witness with our spirit that we are children of God* – Romans 8:16 (said by the Apostle Paul).

18. This is the reason why He is called 'The Holy Spirit' and not 'the Holy Soul'. He is not a soulish being – He is a spirit being from the Divine realm, and His presence restores a person so that he can once again function in fellowship with God by faith and not by sight.

19. To Catholics, being 'born again' means Baptism followed by Confirmation, followed by continual attending the Mass and receiving the Eucharist, followed by often-seeking Reconciliation and performing Penance. Then, we are given new spiritual instincts, a 'new nature' – having a desire for God-centeredness (the thoughts and mind of Christ) instead of self-centeredness.

20. Care must be taken to understand that if the interaction is not harmonious, then bidirectional love is not present. Interaction with God in an impure or unclean manner is actually interaction with the devil. There is no harmony and there is no love by the person. The existence of harmony and love is a free-choice decision. However, the love of God towards the person is unshakable. Regardless of the degree of one's lack of love and harmony, God still loves that person fully and unwaveringly.

21. Reference Genesis 1:28-29 and 2:16-17. Adam and Eve were given dominion over the earth and charged with its care. But in return, they had to praise God by obeying His commands (specifically, the command to not eat from the Tree of the Knowledge of Good and Evil – which, of course, they failed to do – with the resulting fall from grace and establishment of the 'original sin').

22. Reference Genesis 9:1-17. Note that God promises not to destroy all bodily creatures ever again (with the rainbow in the sky as the binder to the promise), and in return, requires that humans not shed human blood, and not eat living animals (to which an accounting will one day be made).

23. Reference Genesis 15: 5 and 15:18-20. Noteworthy is the fact that to bind the covenant, the males had to be circumcised – every male, including house-born slaves and foreign slaves purchased with money (Genesis 17:10-14).

24. Reference Exodus 6:2-8.

25. the Assyrian and Babylonian captivities

26. Isaiah 7:14, Isaiah 11:1-5, 10, and Matthew 1:18-23

27. John 1:1-17

7 - THE SOUL AND SPIRIT IN HISTORY

This pathfinder lineage of Adam and Eve was initiated and championed by God (through interventions and covenants) over terrestrial time, with the aim of bringing this new creature, less than 100% perfect, into the spiritual fold of the divine heavenly realm as efficiently as possible. This is the lineage of Adam, Seth, Enoch, Noah, Shem, Abraham, and eventually leading to Jesus, the Christ and Savior for all humanity. Along the way, other lineages would break off and follow in parallel, but this pathfinder lineage was given a 'jump-start' and monitored closely.

THE TIME BEFORE ADAM AND EVE

It should be emphasized that in this worldview, the time from the physical creation of our universe to the appearance ('birth' or 'creation') of Adam and Eve, is not just a few days. It is billions of years. There are many ways in which the word 'day' (that appears in the Genesis 1-2 creation story) can be interpreted,[1] but from the strictly scientific standpoint, our universe began with the Big Bang about 13.8 billion years ago. The Earth formed about 4.6

billion years ago and the very first life-form appeared between 4.28 and 3.77 billion years ago. Dinosaurs lived 230-65 million years ago, and mammals first appeared about 68 million years ago. The first hominid primates appeared some 6 million years ago, and the first human-like creatures of the genus Homo show up around 2.4 million years ago. Homo-sapiens, anatomically similar to us, first appear about 160,000 years ago, and by 50,000 years ago, behaviorally modern variants of these homo-sapiens are present. Behaviorally modern 'but gracile' variants appear by 12,000 years ago, and the civilizations from which Adam and Eve emerged, arise shortly thereafter.

The Paleolithic Period, or Old Stone Age, and the Mesolithic Period, or Middle Stone Age, have come and gone. The glaciers of the last great Ice Age have receded and the warming trend of the Holocene geologic and climatic era is well underway. It is the time of a New Stone Age, the Neolithic Period, and radical changes are starting to occur. For a good overview of the chronology, refer to *History Before Adam and Eve,* that is included as Appendix B.

A good estimate for the year in which Adam and Eve appear on earth is somewhere between 6032 and 5491 BC.[2] This is based on the premise that God revealed to Adam and Eve, shortly after their expulsion from the Garden of Eden, that their bodies, soul, and spirit would be renewed – and live again in peace and harmony as they did for the first 7 years in the Garden – in another 5½ days, or 5500 years.[3] The correspondence between 5½ days and 5500 years is illustrated by the 'simile' presented in 2 Peter 3:8, where it is said, *But do not ignore this one fact, beloved, that with the Lord one day is like a thousand years and a thousand years like one day.*

Also see Psalms 90:4, *A thousand years in your eyes are merely a day gone by.*[4]

THE TIME OF ADAM TO THE TIME OF NOAH

Adam and Eve were originally hominid creatures without an activated spirit, but they were 'chosen' by God to receive the gift of an advanced transcendent soul and an ethereal activated spirit [5]–they were 'enlightened'. Of course, with the 'Fall' in the Garden of Eden, their spirits were veiled and they were destined to struggle against sin for the rest of their lives (by trying to prevent the veil from falling down too far and trying to raise it when it did fall – and allowing God to enter, and not Satan, with the veil sufficiently raised).[6] Sin was in their nature – and their children inherited their nature. But they fought against the tendency to sin, they asked forgiveness when they did sin, and they maintained a closeness with God – they sought righteousness, and they remained 'enlightened'.

Now, when the spirit of a person has become degraded to the point where he/she has lost much favor with God (the veil has been significantly lowered and is not being raised again), then his/her spirit is said to be clouded.[7] Satan has entered their spirit and tempts them mercilessly.[8] They give in to the tendency to sin and they rarely seek forgiveness. Their righteousness is shady and their enlightenment is reduced. They lose favor with God.

Such is the case to the extreme with Adam and Eve's son Cain. Through his own willful actions, he let the veil of the spirit fall, and could not raise it back up. Satan entered his spirit with a vengeance and tormented his soul.[9] The Holy Spirit could not enter through the veil once it was lowered, and Cain was doomed. He killed his righteous brother Abel out of jealousy and was unable to seek forgiveness in a humble contrite manner. His spirit had become so sealed off, that his righteousness was lost and his enlightenment was greatly reduced – simply put, he lost favor with God. And sadly, most of his children suffered from the same woeful condition.[10]

With the birth of Seth, the condition of the human family is invigorated. There is hope for a reconciliation with God and re-entrance into the divine family. Seth is pure of heart, mind, soul, and spirit. He rejects temptation and maintains a close fellowship with God, obeying the moral imperatives, and giving praise and thanks (through prayer and sacrifice) whenever possible. He keeps the veil of the spirit mostly open – its cloudiness is minimal – and he keeps the devil at bay. He becomes a figurehead of righteousness and the 'guiding light' for God's 'chosen people'.[11]

The Chosen People

Although all people who are descended from Adam and Eve possess a God-given ethereal activated spirit, they are not all on the pathway to holiness because of the damning effect of sinfulness that has resulted from 'the Fall'. The children of Cain were all lost to sin, so God selected Seth to be the 'leading light' (the father) of His 'chosen people' for the purpose of shepherding their journey towards holiness (this is the lineage which He gives the most favor to, and expects the most devoutness from).

But eventually, all of the children of Seth also fall into sin,[12] except for the righteous family of Noah – and God decides to start afresh with a new 'chosen people' by causing a great flood to wipe out all the sinful people, while saving the family of Noah.[13] Thereupon, God chooses Shem, one of the sons of Noah with a mostly pure spirit (the veil was mostly raised; the cloudiness slight), to be the 'leading light' (the father) of His 'chosen people'. Descendants of the other sons of Noah – Ham and Japheth – possess a God-given spirit but it is more clouded, and they are not selected for shepherding.

God later chooses Abraham,[14] and then Isaac – men with a mostly pure spirit – to be the 'leading light' (the father) of His 'chosen people'. Descendants of Ishmael, and the other children of Abraham,[15] also possess a God-given spirit but it is clouded, and they are not selected for shepherding. Unless adulterated by pre-Adamite blood, they all have about the same intrinsic level of soul and spirit fidelity. But this is not certain.[16]

The storyline is similar as we move closer to modern times. At many stages along the way, the group of 'chosen people' fall away and become morally and piously corrupt (the veil has fallen far down; the cloudiness become severe) for one reason or another, and Satan has taken charge. The Hebrew priests establish a religious law with more and more rules, in an attempt to slow down the overall slide into infidelity (and divide the 'fallen' from the 'unfallen'), but it doesn't work because the priests themselves become hypocritical and boastful, further estranging the people.[17]

At certain key times, God chooses a new leader to be the 'leading light' of His new group of 'chosen people', to better shepherd them in the way of righteousness. This, then, is the history of the lineage of Jacob, Joseph, Moses, David, Solomon, and many others – a history of mostly falling away, but always with a few glimmers of holiness and revival – a genealogy eventually leading to Jesus Christ, the Savior of all humanity.[18]

The Partitioning of Humanity

In the year 5000 BC, after the appearance of Adam and Eve and the birth of Seth,[19] the earth is considered to be divided into three parts – that ruled by the family of the holy Seth, that ruled by the family of the unholy Cain, and that ruled by the primitive unenlightened humanoids (the pre-Adamites). But in reality, there is mixing.[20]

So, at this time, with respect to 'holiness' or 'enlightenment', there exist four types of 'human' creature on planet Earth:

1) *The 'enlightened beings with tainted soul and activated but thinly veiled spirit'* – these are the human beings who have inherited an advanced soul and God-centered active spirit from Adam and Eve, who were given the gift direct from God. These are the direct blood descendants of Seth – the tribal group of people who will become the Hebrews, as well as some other tribal groups.

They are mostly pastoral farmers and herders, centered around the greater Mesopotamian region. They have a God-given moral conscience. Their concept of the moral dilemma between right and wrong is driven by strong spiritually reasoned beliefs, and they have a personal relationship with the true, single, all-powerful, invisible God. They have remained (for the most part) in covenant with God and followed His moral commandments.

These people possess an advanced soul and robust spirit in the 'image of God', that have been God-given through the ancestral conduit of Adam and Eve, much like the lump-sum gift of a jump-start. However, the pureness (spotlessness) of soul and spirit has become tarnished because of 'The Fall' (the spirit has been veiled; the soul has been tainted), driven by the existence of 'original sin', and a 'free-will' that is slightly biased and readily amenable to decision-making contrary to the will of God (concupiscence). However, they have willfully controlled the veil of the spirit – keeping it open to allow God to enter while minimizing Satan's presence. They have maintained a sense of righteousness and are 'in-favor' with God. These are the people that God has chosen for his initial relationship with humanity (some might say an experiment) – the people He monitors closely to assess their holiness or their worldliness, their God-centeredness or their self-centeredness – the avatars of a hopefully more encompassing future relationship. They are His 'chosen people'.

2) The 'unenlightened beings with primitive soul and non-activated spirit' – these are the humanoid beings who have not inherited an advanced soul or God-centered active spirit from Adam and Eve. These are the direct blood descendants of the 'pre-Adamites', the primitive hominids who were alive at the time of Adam and Eve's appearance about 5500 BC.

These are mostly itinerant hunter-gatherers,[21] and are sparsely spread throughout the world. Their concept of the moral dilemma between right and wrong is driven mostly by instinct and only slightly by reason, and they generally worship multiple false gods related to nature.

They do not have a covenant with the one true God nor are they inclined to follow His moral commandments (and there is minimal chance that they can be convinced to do so). They sin but they don't realize that they are sinning. Their soul may tend toward or away from Godliness depending on culture and environment, although it will develop and progress slowly (evolve) over the following thousands of years.

3) *The 'marginally enlightened beings with cloaked soul and activated but heavily veiled (clouded) spirit'* – these are the human beings who have inherited an advanced soul and God-centered active spirit from Adam and Eve (type 1), but who, through their own free-will, have corrupted their God-given moral conscience, and have degraded to the point where they have lost favor with God – they have lost the status of being with the 'chosen people'. Satan has entered their spirit and the veil has been lowered significantly. They have been reduced almost to the level of an unenlightened being.[22]

These beings possess an advanced soul and robust spirit in the 'image of God' but the pureness has become severely stained (the soul has been cloaked; the spirit has been clouded) – their behavior mimics that of the unenlightened beings by free choice. Their concept of the moral dilemma between right and wrong is confused, and they may worship multiple false gods, no gods, or just give lip service to the one true God. Their sense of righteousness is token and their favor with God is marginal and fleeting. Many of these people are the direct blood descendants of Cain, and some are mixed descendants of Seth and Cain.[23]

4) *The 'minimally enlightened beings with emerging soul and nascent spirit'* – these are the beings who are of mixed heritage – who may have inherited an advanced soul and God-centered active spirit from one parent (usually the morally corrupt of type 3), and less advanced soul and non-activated spirit from the other parent (type 2). As the number of generations increases, and type 4 people mate with type 2, type 3, or other type 4 people, the level of soul and spirit pureness varies depending upon the parentage, but it generally diminishes.

These beings possess a rudimentary level of soul and spirit in the 'image of God'. Their behavior can vary widely, ranging from holiness to worldliness (God-centeredness or self-centeredness) across the spectrum, especially when the negative effects of the 'Fall' are factored in. As time progresses, the number of beings in this category fluctuates as migrations, travel, and social factors affect the parentage. Many of Cain's descendants intermarry with primitive unenlightened hominids.

Human Population and Migrations

The earliest known migrations of proto-human creatures began about 2 million years ago, with the expansion out of Africa by Homo Erectus.[24] This creature dispersed throughout most of the Old World, reaching as far as southeast Asia. This was followed by groups thought to be ancestors of the Denisovans and Neanderthals, about 500,000 years ago. Late variants of Homo Erectus are thought to have survived until about 143,000 years ago. Neanderthals spread across the Near East and Europe, while Denisovans spread across central and east Asia, to southeast Asia and Oceania.[25] Some Neanderthals are thought to have survived until about 33,000 years ago.

Creatures now scientifically classified as Homo-sapiens first appeared in east-central Africa around 195,000 years ago.[26] About 125,000 years ago, anatomically modern variants began to leave Africa in small numbers, later followed by greater numbers in major waves, spreading around the world.[27] Archeological evidence suggests that they travelled by two different routes:

1) north along the Nile River valley, and then across the Red Sea, and east through the Sinai peninsula into modern-day Israel, Syria, and Iraq – and then northeast to the steppes of central Asia

2) east through the present-day straits of Bab-el-Mandeb on the Red Sea in the Horn of Africa (at that time, there was a much lower sea level and narrower extension),[28] crossing into the Arabian peninsula – and then moving north to central Asia and east to the Indian Ocean.

A large number of individual homo-sapiens migrated north along route #1, searching for food and resources, escaping from enemies, or seeking better shelters.[29] These behaviorally modern beings crossed the Red Sea between 70,000 and 50,000 years ago. [30] Other groups of individuals left Africa along route #2 into the Arabian Peninsula. And from these groups, there were several waves of outward expansion close in time, going southeast into India, southeast Asia, and Australia, northeast into central Asia and Siberia, and northwest into Israel and the Levant.[31] Migrating homo-sapiens, called 'Cro-Magnon Man', coming from groups that originally travelled by both route #1 and route #2, spread across Europe about 40,000 years ago, where they interbred with earlier local Denisovan and Neanderthal populations.[32]

The Holocene era began about 12,000 years ago, after the end of the Last Glacial Maximum. Due to favorable climatic conditions, beginning about 9,000 years ago, behaviorally modern 'but gracile' human groups, which had been geographically confined to a particular locale for environmental or topographic reasons, began to migrate en-masse. By this time, most parts of the world have been settled by homo-sapiens. But large areas that had been covered by glaciers were now re-populated. This period sees the transition from the Mesolithic to the Neolithic social era throughout the world's temperate zones.[33] The Neolithic subsequently gave way to the Bronze Age in Old World cultures, and the gradual emergence of the historical record in the Near East beginning around 4,000 BC.

The people living in the Levant, and the Tigris-Euphrates River valley, in 6000 BC, are likely a mix of people who migrated directly from Africa via route #1, and people who migrated indirectly from Africa via route #2 – and then a) dispersed from western India and Persia, after crossing the Arabian Peninsula, and/or b) expanded north directly through the Arabian Peninsula.

By 5500 BC, near to the time of the appearance of Adam and Eve, the number of homo-sapiens alive in the world is about 20 million,[34] and they have spread out over most all of the globe (with the exception of Polynesia, Pacific Ocean remote islands, the Caribbean islands, and the Arctic). The number of homo-sapiens alive in the Tigris-Euphrates River valley is about 50 thousand.[35] So, it is evident that a large number of pre-Adamites exist at this time (although they do possess a rudimentary soul), both in the region around the Garden of Eden and throughout the rest of the world.

The Great Flood

By the time of the great flood of Noah (approximately 3300 BC),[36] most of the Near East region's population is of type 2, 3, or 4, with type 3 predominant. Only a handful of type 1 people remain – almost all of the children of Seth have lost favor with God. They have intermarried with the children of Cain, and with strange beings known as the 'Watchers' (the children of whom are known as the Nephilim).[37] For most people in the region,[38] the soul and spirit are subject to the effects of 'The Fall', resulting in the existence of 'original sin', and a 'free-will' that is slightly biased and readily amenable to decision-making contrary to the will of God. And Satan has entered the spirit of most people and is working his evil trickery and mischief. The level of moral corruption and self-centeredness has become pervasive – and the veil of the spirit has plummeted – leading God to intervene and rebalance the population to allow for a greater overall sense of divine-consciousness among humanity. A great flood occurs in the Near East region, and the only survivors are Noah and his family. The pre-Adamite descendants, the Nephilim,[39] and all the sinful descendants of Seth and Cain living in the region, are killed.

THE TIME OF NOAH TO THE TIME OF JESUS CHRIST

In the 3300 years after the Flood, as the descendants of the sons of Noah spread out into the known world, the level of God-consciousness among humanity slowly starts to degrade once more. Sinfulness and paganism become prevalent.

The Generations of Noah

The 'Generations of Noah', also called the 'Table of Nations',[40] is a genealogy of the sons of Noah,[41] and their dispersion into many lands after the Flood, focusing on the major known societies of the time. The listing purports to describe all humankind, but in reality, it is restricted to people living in the Egyptian lands, the Mesopotamian lands, Anatolia/Asia Minor, and the Greek Ionian region.

As Christianity later spreads across the Roman Empire, it carries the idea that all people are descended from Noah. But the traditional identification of the ancestry of various peoples concentrated only on the Eastern Mediterranean and the Ancient Near East. It is noteworthy that right up until the 19th century, Shem was associated with all of Asia, Ham with all of Africa, and Japheth with all of Europe.

But this became increasingly problematical. Not all Near Eastern people were covered, and Northern European peoples (the 'barbarians') who existed in late Roman and Medieval times (such as the Celtic, Slavic, Germanic, and Nordic peoples) were not covered at all – nor were other of the world's peoples (such as sub-Saharan Africans, Native Americans, and inhabitants of Central Asia, the Indian subcontinent, the Far East, and Australasia).

Modern analyses have modified the dispersion apportionment slightly, but the link to many of the world's peoples who live remote from the region covered by the Genesis 'Table of Nations', is tenuous at best. Even if some of these links are valid,[42] it still doesn't account for all the people in the world.

The 'Table of Nations', written about the time of Moses, indicates that all people have a common ancestor and place of beginning.[43] But the reality of it is that there are many more people in the world at the time of Moses, than can be accounted for by the genealogy of the 'Table of Nations'. From the time of Noah to the time of Moses is only about 2000 years. But the human race was already spread out over most of the earth (in different races and with different languages) by the time of Moses.

At the time of the Flood, the world population was about 12 million. At the time of Moses, the world population was about 39 million. Could 16 or 17 couples cause a population increase of 27 million in 2000 years, and disperse all over the world? Probably not.[44] But they could account for a major portion of the greater Near East population.

In the year 5 BC,[45] because of the effects of the flood, normal social evolution, mixed race intermingling, and free-will moral corruption, unfettered conscious decision-making, either contrary or obedient to the will of God, exists for most all people in the greater Near East region. Most people range in holiness from 'partially enlightened with cloaked soul and clouded spirit' (type 3) to 'marginally enlightened with emerging soul and nascent spirit' (type 4). The people who are 'enlightened with tainted soul and veiled spirit' (type 1) are few and far between.[46] And since only a small number of unenlightened beings remain in isolated regions,[47] where social evolution progressed slowly with no outside interaction, the number of type 2 people in the region is very small.

However, throughout the rest of the world, type 2 and type 4 people predominate. The more remote, the more likely the people are type 2.

As the level of soul and spirit fidelity decreases in the general population (and in the 'chosen people' monitored by God), the level of moral corruption and self-centeredness increases – until it once again begins to become pervasive. Every individual is different, of course, but on average, the degree to which the veil of the spirit has been lowered, is significant enough to warrant the need for a messiah – and a direct interaction by God. This finally results in the appearance of Jesus Christ and the divine plan to bring salvation to all people of all ancestry.

The major classifying characteristic (discriminating factor) among people, at this time in history, is the degree to which their God-centered moral consciousness has become degraded to a self-centered moral consciousness – the degree to which the veil of the spirit has been lowered.

The Birth of Jesus Christ

It is time for a major miracle to occur.

It is the time when our Lord Jesus Christ – true God and true man – enters into the world, with a mission to usher forth a new ministry of grace – a new mechanism by which the veil of the spirit can be raised, allowing the Holy Spirit to enter and saturate the human spirit. By this act of grace, each individual now has an equal opportunity to partake in the fruits of heaven, by simply believing in good faith that Jesus Christ is his true Lord and Savior.

With the birth, ministry, death, and resurrection of Jesus Christ – and the coming of the Holy Spirit (for infusion into all people with an activated human spirit who truly seek Him and are open to His presence), most people in the Near East and surrounding regions now have an activated spirit and a similar fidelity of soul [48]– all people are designated as His 'chosen people' – and the salvific process begins, where most all people have a chance to obtain salvation and everlasting life through the gift of grace, regardless of their state of holiness.

The classification of type 2 people disappears. All people now have a human spirit – and many people have an activated spirit that is subject to 'original sin' and the effects of the 'Fall'. For most people in the Near East and surrounding areas, the discriminating factor is whether their spirit has become awakened or not. The spirit is awakened when it learns about the Gospel of Jesus Christ and is receptive to the infusion of the Holy Spirit.[49] This most readily occurs with Christian baptism, when the person joins the 'family' of God.

THE TIME OF JESUS CHRIST TO THE PRESENT

Per the 'Great Commission', The Gospel of Jesus Christ is now evangelized to all human beings regardless of the fidelity of their soul and spirit – or their state of holiness – such that all people will have the opportunity to accept Jesus Christ as their personal savior, and thereby receive salvation and a share of everlasting life in harmony and peace in heaven.

The age of evangelism begins. Christian missionaries spread throughout the whole world, bringing the 'Good News' of Jesus Christ to all people. The barbarians of northern Europe are Christianized, as are many people in Africa, the Near East, the Mediterranean, and even the Far East.

This effort does not come easy. Starting with the Apostles (especially Paul, the greatest apostolic missionary) and moving right up until the present day, missionaries have often been met with fierce and deadly resistance. People steeped in pagan rituals (like the Romans), ancient philosophic beliefs (Buddhism, Hinduism), new religions (Islam), and no religion (atheism, communism) have all severely persecuted Christian missionaries [50] – and, make no mistake about it, persecution continues to this very day.[51] But Christianity gradually gains a bigger and wider footprint, and many people have been saved, who would not otherwise have been.

However, the problem in the New World is different. Unlike many of the people in the Old World, these people are not descendants of Noah, and their spirits have not been activated.[52] Trying to awaken a non-activated spirit is different than for awakening an activated spirit. A willful baptism is generally enough to awaken an activated spirit, who already has a rudimentary knowledge and appreciation for the one true God – and this can be accomplished through preaching and teaching. But to save the soul of a person with a non-activated spirit, a different approach is needed. One needs to break the chains of culture and tradition – preaching and teaching are generally insufficient. They need a knowledge and appreciation for the one true God. This is difficult to do, especially when the culture and tradition is very different from that of the Christian missionary. Pockets of success were often offset by stiff resistance and widespread failure.

Thankfully, direct divine intervention has aided the task, and allowed for an easier and smoother transition – with this gift, the spirit can now be activated and awakened almost simultaneously and without excess instruction, coercion, ceremony, or fanfare. The knowledge and appreciation of God suddenly blossom. This is exactly what happened with the appearance of Our Lady of Guadalupe in Tepeyac (Mexico City) in 1531, and in a number of other sites in the Americas and the Far East.[53] The Marian apparition has broken the chains of stale culture and tradition, and allowed for enlightenment through the appreciation of God and Christian baptism.

For the early European explorers of the New World, evangelization of the natives was one of their primary goals, in addition to finding gold, natural resources, and new trade routes. Priests and missionaries were on every ship and in every settlement. There was a sincere desire to Christianize the native people through baptism, thereby awakening their human spirit and enabling them to receive the Holy Spirit. After all, spreading the Gospel to the ends of the earth was the command of Jesus Christ Himself.[54] But, this proved to be easier said than done – there were lots of problematic cultural details because their human spirit had not been activated – and tons of misery and sorrow have unfortunately resulted on both sides. Many missionaries have been martyred, and many native Americans killed, in the quest to spread the Gospel.

For the indigenous pagans of the New World, accepting Christianity – even with the promises of eternal life and forgiveness of sins – was both difficult and dangerous. Believing in just one all-powerful and invisible God was a completely alien concept. For many thousands of years, they had worshipped the sun god, the rain god, the moon god, and the fertility god. Their morals were loosely based on tribal instincts. There were visible manifestations of all this, and it was the fabric of their life and culture.[55] What the Europeans brought seemed like imaginary and foolish nonsense. They faced ridicule and ostracization by their tribe if they accepted the new religion, but they also faced hostility by the Europeans if they rejected it. The result was a lot of misery and sorrow on both sides.[56]

Thank God for the intercession of the Blessed Virgin Mary.

Intercession of the Blessed Virgin Mary

The indigenous pagans of the New World (and many in the Far East, Eastern Asia, Oceana, sub-Saharan western Africa, and other remote regions in the world),[57] whose bloodline had never been touched by the ancestors of Noah (their bloodline was pure pre-Adamic) were without an activated human spirit. They had a soul with a tribal-based morality and a belief system, but could not commune with the one true God.

But the love and mercy brought by Jesus Christ and the Blessed Virgin Mary has changed the way of the world. Once a miraculous apparition becomes revealed, and understood and valued for its significance, the spirit becomes activated and easily awakened by the church through baptism. The knowledge and appreciation of the one true God is now available to almost everyone through enlightened evangelization.

Nearly all people on earth now have an activated spirit and the propensity for the awakening of that spirit. Only a very small number of extremely remote hunter-gatherer cultures remain today that have not been touched by Christian missionaries or divine intervention.[58] And they are rapidly diminishing as westerners and outsiders discover their remote locations.

Salvation Prospective

At the present time, with respect to potential for salvation, there exist five types of 'human' creature on planet Earth:

1) *The 'enlightened'* – the human spirit has been activated and is awakened through Christian baptism, and sanctified by entering of the Holy Spirit – it is thinly veiled and the Holy Spirit presence is strong. These are pious Christians with sanctifying grace and broad sacramental grace.[59] Their salvation is highly likely.

2) *The 'partially enlightened'* – the human spirit has been activated and is awakened through Christian baptism, and sanctified by entering of the Holy Spirit – but it is considerably veiled (clouded), and the Holy Spirit presence is weak. These are irreverent Christians with sanctifying grace but short on sacramental grace. Their salvation is problematical and may entail an extended separation from God in purgatory.

3) *The 'marginally enlightened'* – the human spirit has been activated and is awakened through monotheistic, but non-Christian, religious rites, but is not sanctified since the Holy Spirit has not entered – it is significantly veiled. These may be Noahic non-Christians of Abrahamic lineage (Jews, Samaritans, and Muslims, descendants of Shem).[60] They may not be consciously aware of the Gospel, or they may be aware but willfully choose to reject it.[61] Their salvation is possible but not assured; it is in divine providence.

4) *The 'minimally enlightened'* – the human spirit has been activated but not awakened because of polytheistic or pagan religious convictions – it is heavily veiled. These may

be Noahic non-Christians <u>not</u> of Abrahamic lineage (descendants of Ham and Japheth), with perhaps a very small number of Sethites or Cainites who survived the great Flood. As with type 3, they may not be consciously aware of the Gospel, or they may be aware but willfully choose to reject it. Their salvation is not assured; it is in divine providence.

5) *The 'unenlightened'* – the human spirit has not been activated, or is only partially (or intermittently) activated. These may be the descendants of pre-Adamites, and mixtures of surviving Sethites or Cainites with pre-Adamites. Their salvation is not assured; it is in divine providence and a great mystery.

There is also a sixth category that could be added called 'once enlightened but now unenlightened' – these are people who at one time were classified as type 1, 2, or 3, but because of willful conviction, have disavowed their belief in the one true God and the promises of God. Their spirit was once awakened (and possibly sanctified), but by their own 'free-will', they have veiled their spirit so heavily that there is no longer a significant presence of the Holy Spirit, although at one time there may have been. It's just as if the spirit had not been awakened. A reversal of the will is always possible, resulting in opening (or raising) the veil, and allowing the Holy Spirit to regenerate. But unless the will is reversed, the salvation of these people is very doubtful.

On the flip side, it is possible that people once classified as type 3, 4, or 5, could be evangelized and elevated to type 1 or type 2. With the proper evangelization and with God's grace, even type 5 people can be elevated and saved. Thus, the importance of continued evangelization efforts, especially in the 'non-Christian' regions of the world.

NOTES

---

1. The exact definition of a 'day' in Genesis 1-2 is a matter of some debate among theologians. At opposite ends of the spectrum are roughly 24 earth hours (or the time between successive sunsets) according to literalists, and millions of years (per the 'framework interpretation' of scientific cosmological evolution) according to non-literalists. However, a 'day' could also be a Divine 'day' (or a distinguishable increment of the Divine 'Now'), where 'evening' and 'morning' are simply the earthly terms that enable a relative level of human understanding of the Divine 'Now'

2. This is based on assuming that the upper limit on the death of Jesus is 36 AD, the lower limit on the birth of Jesus is 6 BC, Adam and Eve were both 20 years old when they were placed in the Garden of Eden by Divine intervention, and they were in the Garden for 7 years.

3. The reference for this can be found in the following works of the pseudepigrapha: Rutherford H. Platt Jr. (ed), *The Forgotten Books of Eden;* (New York: Alpha House, 1926); and S. C. Malan, D.D., Vicar of Broadwindsor (trans.), *The Conflict of Adam and Eve with Satan; A Book of the early Eastern Church;* translated from the Ethiopic, with Notes from the Kufale, Talmud, Midrashim, and other Eastern Works; (London: Williams and Norgate, 1882).

4. Of course, the 'Fall' of Adam and Eve meant that the appearance of humanity in the image of God, pure in body, soul, and spirit, would have to wait for a Messiah (a new Adam) who would, through grace, subsume the imperfectness (sins) of the finite human creature and provide him with an opportunity for salvation and return to the Divine. Whether 5½-6 days, or 5500-6000 years, that is the time from the appearance of the chosen humanoid creature Adam, to the appearance of the Christ, the new Adam, fully God and fully human, pure in body, soul, and spirit, and 'The Way' for all human creatures to take their destined places in the hierarchy of Divine Spirit.

5. Although both the soul and the spirit are transcendent (they are supernatural - go beyond natural explanations), the spirit is ethereal because it is otherworldly (from the divine realm).

6. Satan hastens the falling of the veil, allowing for mischievous temptations and preventing the Holy Spirit from entering.

7. The degree of cloudiness (or fogginess) of the spirit is directly proportional to the extent that the veil of the spirit has been lowered (lowered all the way = very cloudy; raised all the way = minimally cloudy). And the lower the level of the veil, the harder it is for the Holy Spirit to enter. But even with the veil lowered all the way, a person can still receive the Holy Spirit if he/she wills it hard enough.

8. Note that it's not a question of whether Satan will enter (with some bad luck or probability). If the veil is sufficiently open, he WILL enter. There is no maybe about it. And it happens to all people with a spirit.

9. Satan couldn't fully win over the soul and spirit of Adam and Eve, and so, out of vindictiveness, he went after Cain with a vengeance.

10. The story of Adam and Eve, Cain and Abel, Seth, and all of their children is told in resplendent detail in the following: Edward N Brown, *The Passion of Eve: Remembering the End* (Chicago: Crystal Sea Press, 2020).

11. *At that time men began to invoke the Lord by name* – Genesis 4:26.

12. Many of the children of Seth decide to cohabit with the children of Cain (resulting in the loss of holiness), and many of the children of Seth are corrupted by a group of beings called 'the Watchers' (thought to be fallen angels returning to earth with evil intentions). In fact, the offspring of the Sethites and the Watchers become hideous evil monsters known as the 'Nephilim', and wreak havoc upon the world.

13. Most of the mixed heritage people – those with blood from the line of Cain and the line of Seth – those with blood from the line of Seth and the 'Watchers' (the Nephilim) – and those with blood from the line of Cain and the pre-Adamites – were wiped out by the great flood of Noah. Only Noah's family, from the blood line of Seth, survived (although there may have been others far away, depending on the extent of the flood). [For those detail-minded, the mixed heritages of Seth with pre-Adamites, or Cain with the 'Watchers', is insignificant – there are no known references].

Pure-blood descendants of Cain, the Nephilim, and the pre-Adamites were effectively wiped out. This is the amazing story of Noah's Ark, familiar to people all over the world.

14. In Judaism, Abraham is the founding father of the special relationship between the Jews and God.

15. Abraham had 8 sons and an unknown number of daughters. The sons were: Ishmael by his Egyptian servant Hagar; Isaac by his wife Sarah; and Zimran, Jokshan, Medan, Midian, Ishbak, and Shuah by his concubine Keturah.

16. Although Ishmael was the oldest son of Abraham, Isaac was the first-born son of Abraham's wife Sarah. Therefore, it is known with certainty that she was a blood descendant of Noah, and therefore so was Isaac. The purity of pedigree of Ishmael and Abraham's other 6 sons is less certain since his partner was a foreign concubine. There is a slight possibility of pre-Adamite heritage, and therefore, the possibility of a degraded spirit.

17. Jesus Christ often sermonized about this issue (Refer to: Matthew 6:2,5; Luke 12:1-2).

18. The family blood record of Jesus Christ is given in Matthew 1:1-17. The constant repetition of the term 'was the father of' implies the continuous presence of God in Israel and Judah, sustaining the faith and hope of the people.

19. Seth is thought to have been born about 5424 BC, when Adam and Eve were 130 years old.

20. There is evidence in the Bible for interaction with the primitive hominids – who was Cain afraid would kill him? (Genesis 4:14); who was Cain's wife? (Genesis 4:17); who was Seth's wife? (Genesis 5:6). Although there is the possibility that Cain and Seth married their sisters, who was Cain afraid of, being banished to a strange land? Who did he build a city for?

21. Although some pastoral settlements are beginning to spring up, the pre-Adamites do not have an activated spirit.

22. Some scholars consider them to be a subcategory of type 1.

23. Many of the children of Seth decide to cohabit with the children of Cain (resulting in the loss of holiness), and many of the children of Seth are corrupted by a group of beings called 'the Watchers' (thought to be fallen angels returning to earth with evil intentions).

In fact, the offspring of the Sethites and the Watchers become hideous evil monsters known as the 'Nephilim', and wreak havoc upon the world.

24. Homo Erectus followed the same route out of Africa as later homo-sapiens (via route 1 and route 2).

25. There is evidence that Denisovans interbred with Neanderthals in central Asia where their habitats overlapped.

26. Anatomically modern proto-humans emerged about 300,000 years ago through a merging of populations in east and south-central Africa.

27. It should be noted that early Eurasian fossils that date to about 200,000 years ago, are most likely the failed dispersal attempts by very early homo-sapiens, who were replaced by local Neanderthal populations.

28. The straits of Bab-el-Mandeb lie between Yemen on the Arabian peninsula and Djibouti and Eritrea on the Horn of Africa. The straits connect the Red Sea to the Gulf of Aden. They have been dubbed the 'Gates of Grief' because of the treacherous waters.

29. There is some evidence that Homo-sapiens were reduced to about 10,000 individuals, because of a large volcanic eruption about 74,000 years ago!

30. Around 50,000 years ago the world was entering the last ice age and water was trapped in the polar ice caps, so sea levels were much lower. Today, at its narrowest point, the Red Sea is about 12 miles wide, but 50,000 years ago it was much narrower and sea levels were 230 feet lower. Although the sea was never completely closed off, there may have been small islands which could be reached by simple rafts. There is some evidence that early humans may have crossed the Red Sea in search of sea food obtained by beachcombing.

31. There is speculation that groups of these proto-humans arrived in southern China about 100,000 years ago, and in Australia about 50,000 years ago (in fact, the aborigines of Australia may be the descendants of the first wave of migration out of Africa).

32. Contemporary human populations are descended in small part (below 10% contribution) from regional varieties of archaic Neanderthal and Devonian proto-humans.

33. typically defined as eras of cultural progress or civilization

34. Over the years 6000 BC to 5000 BC, Neolithic culture and technology spread out from the Levant and the Tigris-Euphrates River valley (the 'fertile crescent') into Europe and Asia. However, in much of the rest of the world, people still lived in scattered Paleolithic hunter-gatherer communities. As a result of the Neolithic Revolution, the world population increased sharply, going from about 10 million in 6000 BC to about 40 million people in 5000 BC.

35. In the Neolithic period in Mesopotamia, community settlements that centered around farming, herding, and trading began to take hold. Scattered agrarian settlements grew into larger communities with organized leadership and division of labor. The people developed the earliest form of a written language – cuneiform – with which they kept detailed clerical records. Dating to about 3200 BC, Uruk was the first community recognized as a 'city' (with mud brick houses). It alone, had a population of about 50,000 people. Therefore, this region is known as the 'cradle of civilization'.

36. Many timelines derived from the analysis of many ancient texts and records reveals that 3898-3298 BC is a good estimate for the date of Noah's Flood. This is based on the Greek Septuagint chronology. The Masoretic chronology (which many think has been corrupted) puts the date at 2518 BC. Purely scientific studies have postulated that the flood occurred about 2900 BC.

37.. The 'Watchers' were a foreign group of people who taught the children of Seth the earthly ways of agriculture, crafts, and entertainment. But their teaching caused the children of Seth to want to depart from the ways of God – and they became less God-conscious.

Owing to this close interaction, they intermarried with the Watchers, and then with the children of Cain. The product of a union between a child of Seth and a child of Cain departed even further from the ways of God.

The product of a union between a child of Seth and a Watcher was a monstrous giant, called the Nephilim in the aggregate, who were horrendously sinful. Early religious tradition maintained that the Watchers were fallen angels, and the Nephilim were half-human, half-fallen-angel unnatural beings.

38. Outside the Near East region, most people are type 2, although some of Cain's descendants may have made it to the Far East., resulting in some type 4. Type 2 people are not subject to the effects of 'The Fall,' since they are without an activated spirit.

39. The descendants of the Nephilim, the Elioud, are also killed.

40. Genesis 10

41. After the flood, Shem had 5 sons, Ham had 4 sons, and Japheth had 7 sons. According to many ancient writings, Noah had a fourth son who was born after the Flood, named Bouniter (or Maniton), but his children are unknown.

42. Some scholars maintain that the people of southern Africa, Germany, the Balkans, and Greece are sprung from Japheth. Others suggest that the people of Persia, Russia, China, and Japan also descend from Japheth. Similar claims put Ham as the father of Egypt, Arabia, and Canaan, and Shem as the father of the Native American peoples, eastern Persia, India, and southeast Asia. But all of this is very speculative.

43. There are 70 names listed in the Table of Nations. Many scholars believe that these 70 names express symbolically the unity of humanity – corresponding to the 70 descendants of Israel who go down into Egypt with Jacob, per Genesis 46:27 – and the 70 elders of Israel who visit God with Moses at the covenant ceremony, per Exodus 24:1-9.

44. For comparison, the world population increased from about 800 million in 1 AD to about 6,143 million in 2000 AD.

But, the starting point is much greater (400 million couples instead of 16 couples), and the introduction of medicine and improved living conditions have a pronounced effect.

45. best estimate for the birth of Jesus Christ

46. The parents of the Blessed Virgin Mary (Anne and Joachim), and Mary herself, are representatives of the few purely enlightened type 1 people living at the time (the veil of the spirit being mostly open and Satan being refused entrance).

47. Most pre-Adamites in the Mesopotamian region were killed by the great flood of Noah. But outside this region, there remain some isolated peoples, descended from the pre-Adamites, that do not have a God-given activated spirit, although they may have what appears to be a primitive spirit associated with pagan or nature-gods. However, this spirit is illusory. It is really just a psychological aspect of the soul and not a true active spirit as given by the one true triune God. The primitive soul has evolved to enable this.

Nevertheless, these people can be evangelized, either by missionary work (which occurred extensively in the New World after 1492 AD) or by direct revelation from God (e.g., Marian apparitions), and a God-conscious spirit can be infused into their very being. In addition, their primitive soul has evolved over time, giving it a higher fidelity (although probably still lower than an 'enlightened' being), further enabling evangelization efforts (if done properly).

48. although there are still some isolated remote peoples who have a soul fidelity that is somewhat less than the worldwide average because of societal restrictions, and the lack of outside information and influences

49. Positive receptivity is the default state. That's one reason why babies are baptized. Their spirit is activated and receptive. Older unbaptized people may be less receptive if their spirit has been contaminated by the devil.

50. Non-religious persecution has been, and still is, a major sorrow. People afraid of new ways because of perceived loss of leadership power, personal esteem, or economic wealth, can drive severe persecutions.

A good early example is the aggression against Gaius and Aristarchus (traveling companions of Paul) in the 'Riot of the Silversmiths' in Ephesus (Reference: Acts 19:23-40).

51. More people have been martyred in the history of the world simply because they are Christians than for any other cause or reason. It is estimated that more than 70 million Christians have been martyred over the last two millennia, more than half of which died in the 20th century under fascist and communist regimes. Reference: Todd M. Johnson, "Christian Martyrdom: Who? Why? How?", *Gordon Conwell Theological Seminary*, 2019. Credible research has revealed that every year an estimated 100,000 Christians are killed because of their faith (although some have postulated the number is closer to 10,000). The truth of it all is that 2/3 of the 2.3 billion Christians in the world today live in dangerous neighborhoods. They are often poor, and belong to ethnic, linguistic, and cultural minorities. And they are often at grave risk.

52. There may yet be a salvific remediation for people who did not possess a human spirit (pre-Adamites before the passion of Christ) or did not have an activated human spirit (pre-Adamites after the passion of Christ), if one digs deep into the dogma of faith. It is possible that even beings without an infused spirit can come to a knowledge of God by reasoning from the created world. The Catholic Church teaches that sufficient grace is offered to all souls, and that God will not turn away those who do everything within their power to find God and live according to His law. Luke 16:22 speaks of the 'bosom of Abraham', which is understood as a temporary state of souls awaiting entrance into Heaven. The 'Limbo of the Fathers' (or 'Limbo of the Patriarchs') is seen as the temporary state of those who, despite the sins they may have committed, die in the friendship of God, but cannot enter Heaven until the redemptive power of Jesus Christ makes it possible.

53. Other good examples of Marian appearances in the Americas occurred with 'Our Lady of the Good Event', 1594-1634 in Quito, Ecuador; 'Our Lady of Cuapa', 1980 in San Francisco de Cuapa, Nicaragua; 'Our Lady of the Rosary of San Nicolas', 1983-1990 in San Nicolas de los Arroyos, Buenos Aires, Argentina; and 'Mary, Virgin and Mother, Reconciler of all Peoples and Nations', 1984 in Finca Betania, Miranda, Venezuela.

Other non-European examples of Marian appearances, to help save the people of far-flung remote areas, occurred with 'Our Lady of Good Health', 1570 and 1587 in Velankanni, Tamil Nadu, India; 'Our Lady of La Vang', 1798 in Hai Lang, Quang Tri, Vietnam; 'Our Lady of Good Help', 1859 in Champion, Wisconsin, USA; 'Our Lady of China', 1900 in Donglu, Hebei, China; 'Our Lady of Akita', 1973 in Yuzawadai, Akita, Japan; and 'Our Lady of Kibeho', 1981-1983 in Kibeho, Rwanda. Of course, Marian appearances have also occurred in Europe when the holiness of the people have fallen dramatically.

54. Matthew 28:19-20; Acts 1:8

55. The culture of the indigenous Americans was very different from that of the pagan Europeans. They looked different, acted different, and they had not been gradually visited by traders, explorers, and missionaries. In retrospect, this should have warranted a different approach to evangelization.

56. Not to be overlooked is that the Europeans brought guns (which, of course, the natives feared but thought desirable), African slaves, and new diseases (which, unfortunately, ravaged the natives, who had no immunity – in fact, many diseases brought by the Africans, affected both the Europeans and the native Americans).

57. most notably, the hinterlands in the Far East, Peloponnesia, and Oceana.

58. The most prominent of these primitive societies are the African bushmen, the Australian aboriginals, and the Papuans of New Guinea (the latter who have a high percentage of Denisovan in their DNA).

59. Sacramental grace is the interior grace received through a sacrament. It is a special type of sanctifying grace intended to aid the recipient in fulfilling the obligations and purpose of the sacrament more perfectly. For example, in the Holy Eucharist, our souls are nourished and united with God. And in Penance, we can expiate our sins and make a sincere effort to amend our lives and abstain from future sins.

60. A further breakdown can be made between descendants of Isaac (the Jews), descendants of Ishmael (the Muslims), and descendants of Abraham's other sons, but a distinct classification according to salvation prospective is difficult.

61. Those who are aware of the Gospel but willfully choose to reject it will have a much harder time finding salvation. For those who have never been made aware of the Gospel, there may be a salvific remediation. The situation is similar to that of not possessing a human spirit (before Christ) or not having an activated human spirit (after Christ). See Endnote 52. The Catholic Church teaches that sufficient grace is offered to all souls, and that God will not turn away those who do everything within their power to find God and live according to His law.

SUMMARY AND TAKE-AWAY

The body of a human being is 'human' precisely because it is infused with a spiritual soul.[1] The human being is unique among living creatures because, in reality, a human being is a created immortal spirit that is united with, and imbues, a material body. In other words, the human being is the only creature with a body, whose soul is integrated with a spirit. Adam and Eve were the first creatures on earth to have an integrated soul and spirit.

The spirit, when contrasted with the soul, refers to those aspects of human life and activity that transcend our physical bodily limitations – this opens the soul up to the possibility of a supernatural life in the grace of God.

By the design of God, the human being is destined to have a supernatural end to his material life on earth. The design is such that the supernatural end may be either eternal communion with God (heaven) or eternal separation from God (hell). If a person willfully believes in the grace of God, and receives the blessing of God into his heart, then his soul and his spirit will be elevated to the divine domain of heaven for eternal communion with God, even though his thoughts and deeds while living on earth make him undeserving of such a gift.

The greatest gift that can possibly be imagined – the gift of life in the 'image of God' – has been made available to all people living today on planet earth. But the gift has to be accepted by the soul and the spirit (the heart and mind inclusive). God has given us a soul and a spirit with which we can maintain, develop, appreciate, and seek understanding of this magnificent world, but also so that we can eventually experience the next magnificent world.

We can try to do this on our own (through meditation, mysticism, or theosophy) without accepting the gift from God. We can reflect on our own consciousness, love and relate to the others around us, and interact with an imaginary energy force or entity. But one can only interact with the true creator God of all reality in a compassionate, loving, and devotional relationship, IF one accepts the gift of life in the 'image of God'. This entails the awakening of an activated human spirit, and the resulting infusion of the presence of the Holy Spirit. It is not difficult, but it involves a choice – to accept the gift or not. There are various approaches for trying to do this, but the 'gold standard' is through the belief, obedience, and heeding of the Christian doctrine.

The Christian doctrine involves the concepts of creation and redemption, where the concept of creation is inseparably linked to the concept of redemption. Only if the existence of creation is good, and only if human trust in creation is fundamentally justified, are human beings at all redeemable. In other words, only if the Redeemer is also the Creator, can He really be a Redeemer.[2]

Creation and redemption are part of reality. And all reality is ultimately defined by the Christian concept of God

– the Holy Trinity – the one, only, and 'true' God, who is a Being supreme in a relationship of pure agape love. All relationships have to be based on the recognition of this 'truth'. The Christian God is the ultimate absolute Truth. And Truth is that which corresponds to 'Reality' as it actually is, and not as we humans, in our finite limited physical shells, construct or imagine it to be. Pointers, hints, signs, and clues come to us in language, images, experience, awareness, reasoning, dreams, and revelation. All are forms of information transfer and information processing. For lack of a better explanation, we classify this information as evidence and relate it to reality under the rubric of 'words'. That is why, *In the beginning was the Word, and the Word was with God, and the Word was God.*[3] [John 1:1]. The answer to everything is right there.

NOTES

---

1. Catechism of the Catholic Church, paragraphs 363-364

2. Pope Benedict XVI (Joseph Ratzinger). *'In the Beginning ...': A Catholic Understanding of the Story of Creation and the Fall*, trans. by Boniface Ramsey (Grand Rapids, MI: William B Eerdmans Publishing Co., 1995).

3. Use of the term 'The Word' (from 'logos' in Greek) nicely combines God's dynamic, creative 'word' (as exemplified in the Book of Genesis), a personified preexistent 'Wisdom' as the instrument of God's creative activity (as exemplified in the Book of Proverbs), and the ultimate intelligibility of reality (as exemplified in Hellenistic philosophy).

APPENDIX A

MYSTICAL CONCEPTS THAT ENLIGHTEN THE SPIRIT

The 12 Fundamental Concepts of Existence:

(1) The essence of all Being (The Great Existent) **IS** the source of ultimate absolute Reality and Truth.

(2) The Christian Trinitarian God is the essence of all Being – the Creator of everything. This is the best explanation for addressing humankind's overarching questions associated with Being, Reality, and Truth (the who, what, when, where, why, and how of everything).

(3) The Creator is the Grand Designer, the instigator and driver behind the existence of a divine Grand Design.

(4) The divine Grand Design is the reason for the existence of Reality as we know it (the universe containing the earth and human beings). The Grand Design contains an objective plan (intended scheme), a specifying blueprint (layouts at various levels of detail), and a concept of operations (implementation plan) for after instantiation (similar to a large-scale engineering project today). It incorporates both deterministic and probabilistic processes.

(5) The intention of, and specification for, the instantiated Grand Design is that space/time and matter/energy would unfold (develop, transform, evolve) naturally according to finely tuned cosmological and physical laws and processes incorporated into the design, such that eventually the environmental conditions would be proper for enabling and sustaining human life.

(6) The intention of, and specification for, the instantiated Grand Design is that matter/energy and data/information (e.g., genetic coding) would unfold (develop, transform, evolve) naturally according to biological and informational laws and processes incorporated into the design, such that eventually life would emerge from non-life, and life forms would develop (evolve) into beings that would be sufficiently mature (in brainpower and cellular processes) that they would be capable of receiving and accommodating the gift of spiritual vigor (an activated spirit) from God – a gift that would turn them into human beings.

(7) The implementation plan for the Grand Design recognized that natural development following probabilistic principles could not assure the desired environmental conditions for enabling and sustaining human life. Therefore, the allowance for divine designer intervention was built into the design, such that adjustments (which could also be called tunings or alterations) could be performed in order to put the process of natural unfolding back on the desired track, and ensure the proper environmental conditions for the emergence of human life (the Anthropic Principle argues that the universe is the way it is because if it was any different, we humans wouldn't be here to ponder it). All the physical laws and processes created are quantitatively fine-tuned to be just right (Anthropic Coincidences). The slightest deviation and human life would not be possible. But, exactly how much of the fine tuning was accomplished after instantiation [the degree of adjustment around the initial design values], and how much before instantiation [the degree of

accuracy of the initial design values], is a mystery that only God has the answer to.

(8) The implementation plan for the Grand Design recognized that natural development following probabilistic principles could not assure the desired creature maturity wherein spiritual vigor could be gifted. Therefore, the allowance for divine designer intervention was built into the design, such that adjustments (which could also be called modifications or amendments) could be performed in order to put the process of natural unfolding back on the desired track, and ensure the desired creature maturity wherein spiritual vigor could be gifted (e.g., the Great Flood of Noah, the Incarnation of the Eternal Word).

(9) Through instillation of the gift of spiritual vigor – an advanced soul and activated spirit – into humanoid 'proto-human' creatures by divine intervention according to the Grand Design plan, human beings in the 'image of God' were created (a fuzzy image, but one that could become more focused through personal relationship with God). The first creatures to receive the gift of spiritual vigor were Adam and Eve (the first creatures designated to start a pathfinder lineage). Seth was the first creature to receive the gift of sanctifying grace.

(10) The soul and spirit fidelity in the human being was divinely adjusted as a result of the 'Fall' of Adam and Eve and the enlightenment of Seth. However, the adjustments now allow for the infiltration of Satan's evil influence into the human spirit – but the influence can be controlled by the individual's free-will.

(11) The overall objective of the Grand Design is that living creatures – human beings, the flagship of creation, and God's beacon on earth (where He can monitor their progress in striving for enlightenment, spiritual truth, and the sharing of divine love) – will eventually evolve to a state sufficiently close to spiritual divinity (they will put Satan behind them), that they will be able to achieve salvation (through justification and sanctification) and reunification with God in the divine spiritual realm.

(12) To ensure that the objective of the Grand Design is met for as many people as possible, the Grand Designer Himself intervened by assuming a human nature, such that the divine nature and the human nature would be personally united in the One Person of the Eternal Word – Jesus Christ – true God and true man. The eternal Second Person of the Trinity came down upon the earth in human form to save us from our sin and redeem all humankind ("The Word became flesh and made His dwelling among us" - John 1:14). As a man, He was able to suffer and die, such that salvation through grace and eternal life would be available to all people.

Corollaries to the Fundamental Concepts:

(1) God has provided human beings with three 'methodologies' to help in our understanding of Reality: a) the deductive 'method' of understanding natural phenomena – revealed to us through investigative experiment and inferential reasoning (science)

b) the inductive 'method' of understanding natural phenomena – revealed to us through creative synthesis and inventive reasoning (design/art), and

c) the visionary 'method' of understanding both natural and supernatural phenomena – revealed to us through reflective contemplation and insightful reasoning (philosophy).

(2) Since God is the 'author' (guiding-hand, wisdom-giver, or inventor) of all three 'methodologies', the resulting understanding must agree when properly interpreted through the lens of theology.

(3) Being, Reality, and Truth are best understood by human beings as a metaphysical cosmology integrating theological aspects with the deductive, inductive, and philosophical aspects. The 'books' of Holy Scripture, which are revealed to us through divine revelation and providence, are the cornerstone of theological reasoning and the basis for fully understanding all Being, Reality, and Truth.

Inferences from the Fundamental Concepts:

(1) Geological evidence for an old earth is reliable.

(2) Animals lived and died long before the 'Fall' of Adam and Eve.

(3) Humanoids lived and died before the 'Fall' of Adam and Eve.

(4) The Great Flood of Noah was a real historical event, but was localized and not global.

(5) Most fossils are relics of organisms that lived and died before human beings appeared.

(6) Human beings are defined holistically rather than anthropologically

The Overarching Fundamental Concept:

Because human beings are finite corporeal creatures existing in a special space/time realm, we can never fully know the absolute truth about anything – **EXCEPT** one thing: – that the one true Almighty Trinitarian God – source of all Truth, creator of all existence, redeemer of just souls, and the fountain of agape love – does in fact exist, and is the essence of all Being and the focus of all Reality.

APPENDIX B

HISTORY BEFORE ADAM AND EVE

(BYA = billion years ago; MYA = million years ago;
TYA = thousand years ago)

13.798 BYA (± 37 million years or thereabouts), the universe begins with the occurrence of the Big Bang.

4.6 BYA, the planet Earth forms from an accretion disc of gas and dust revolving around a young Sun.

4.5 BYA, the Moon is formed when the Earth collides with another planetary object, sending a large number of moonlets into orbit around the young Earth - which eventually coalesce to form the Moon. The gravitational pull of the new Moon stabilizes the Earth's fluctuating axis of rotation and sets up the favorable conditions for life to begin and develop.

3.9 BYA, life first appears on the Earth (archaea) as primitive simple cells without a nucleus (prokaryotes).

[The abiogenesis of life (life from non-life) was a miraculous event and present-day science cannot describe exactly how it happened.[1] It was in God's design from the beginning that life would begin, develop, and change, but whether the very first life was a direct divine intervention, an indirect divine guidance of natural phenomena, or just natural processes at work per the original divine design, is a question for philosophers and theologians.]

3.5 BYA, bacteria appear, splitting off from archaea.

3 BYA, cyanobacteria appear that can produce oxygen by photosynthesis.

1.8 BYA, green algae, amoeba, and membrane-bound cells (eukaryotes) appear.

1.2 BYA, the earliest sexual reproduction occurs.

800 MYA, multicellular organisms emerge and proliferate.

550 MYA, fungi, sponges, corals, and sea anemones appear.

541 MYA, the tree of life begins to really branch out with the **Cambrian Explosion**. The rate of diversification in the oceans accelerates and the variety of life quickly begins to resemble that of today. Trilobites (now extinct), mollusks, crabs, snails, clams, and worms soon appear. Almost all present-day animal types (phyla) appear during the next 100 million years.

[As with the abiogenesis of life, the Cambrian Explosion may well have been part of God's design from the beginning, but the exact mechanism is unknown.]

434 MYA, the first primitive plants move onto land, followed by jawless fish, ray-fish, spiders, scorpions, and toothed fish.

363 MYA, the Earth begins to resemble its present state. Insects roam the land and will soon take to the skies, sharks swim the oceans as top predators, and vegetation covers the land - with seed-bearing plants and forests soon to flourish. Crabs, ferns, amphibians, reptiles, and beetles appear shortly thereafter.

250 – 66 MYA, animal and plant life, both marine and land, begins to proliferate. Conifers, cycads, flies, turtles, and herbivore dinosaurs appear, followed by the first

pterosaurs, newts, salamanders, and blood-sucking insects.

100 MYA, large dinosaurs, snakes, and bees appear.

80 MYA, ants appear.

68 MYA, the first small mammals appear and the giant predator dinosaurs, like the Tyrannosaurus, are thriving.

66 – 6 MYA, mammals, including the carnivorous variety, slowly become the dominant species, and the dinosaurs quickly die out. Large flightless birds, owls, and the first primate-like mammals appear, followed by modern birds, whales, bats, camels, and butterflies. Grasses begin to diversify and expand. Sloths, eagles, and hawks appear.

55 MYA, the first true primates appear.

35 MYA, monkeys appear.

23 MYA, the first apes appear, followed by deer, giraffes, and bears.

10 MYA, horses appear, and there occurs a major diversification of insects, grassland mammals, and savanna life-forms.

[It should be noted that a number of large-scale extinctions occurred during all of this past time, eradicating many species, like the dinosaurs, and creating new environmental conditions which favored the development of new and different life forms. Again, as with the abiogenesis of life and the Cambrian Explosion, the exact manner in which God's hand was played out in all this

is a great mystery for theologians, philosophers, and scientists to ponder.]

6 MYA, the first species of hominid primate creature to be distinctly different from the chimpanzee (and probably related to the human species) appears. They have adaptations for awkward bipedalism, as well as a larynx that can enable formative speech.

3.9 MYA, the first upright walking ape-like pre-human creatures, vaguely similar to you and me, first appear. Of the genus Australopithecus, they have enlarged jaws, teeth, and chewing muscles.

2.4 MYA, the first somewhat human-like creatures of the genus Homo begin to appear. These creatures have a larger brain ($\sim$600 cc),[2] a more vertical face, and fingers capable of precision grip.

2 MYA, with the development of the ability to make simple stone tools for processing food, the proto-human creatures begin to flourish. They have smaller jaws and cheek teeth than the earlier creatures, but have long legs and arched feet, well-suited for running after big animals. Brain size also increases (to $\sim$800 cc).

1 MYA, the proto-human creatures have developed sophisticated stone flakes and tools for hunting. Brain size increases further (to $\sim$1100 cc).

400 TYA, the Neanderthals appear. They have a brain size almost as large as we have today (up to $\sim$1400 cc). They use wooden spears for hunting and stone cutting tools for food preparation. Their bodies are shorter and stockier than ours, and they have a huge nose for humidifying and warming cold, dry air. They live in

shelters, make and wear clothing, and have rudimentary control of fire.

200 TYA, creatures anatomically similar to modern human beings appear. They hunt wild animals and birds, and collect wild fruits, nuts, and berries. The semi-effective and haphazard control of fire for warmth, protection, and cooking, is in use and integral to their daily life.

160 TYA, a new hominid type creature appears on Earth. It has a very large brain (**up to** 1500 cc),[3] a high and round cranial braincase, high vertical forehead, almost no heavy brow ridges, a well-defined chin, and a small face tucked below the braincase. Most significantly, it possesses the intrinsic capability for tool-making, art, symbolic thought, analytical thought, and full-blown language, the prelude to what can be called consciousness.[4] The species is called Homo Sapiens, and they live concurrently with the Neanderthals.

100 TYA, groups of homo sapiens creatures venture into Israel and the Levant area.

50 TYA, behaviorally modern variants of these homo sapiens creatures suddenly appear. There is a slight increase in brain size, along with augmented memory, information processing, and neuronal functionality. But complexity is the key. Brain complexity is accompanied by increased complexity of the eye and vision system (especially for spatial resolution and psycho-emotional tearing), the larynx and speech system (for articulation), and the pineal gland (for sleep and awareness stages),[5] all meant to foster learning, caring, language, and writing (immortalized

communication). The creatures begin to do things they had never done before – there is a discontinuity in the usually slow process of change – **a great leap forward**. The ability to plan ahead, innovate technologically, establish social and trade networks, adapt to changing environmental conditions, and utilize symbolic communication (language), all suddenly blossom. A rich symbolic consciousness becomes extant.[6]

[It is all part of the grand divine design, and the likelihood of there being a divine intervention of some sort is high. But the details of that intervention are forever hidden from us.]

28 TYA, the homo sapiens creatures, due to ingenuity and adaptability, become the only surviving species of the genus Homo.[7]

12 TYA, behaviorally modern **but gracile** variants appear. A new intensified and controlled level of food collection and production begins to develop. Figs are cultivated. Ritual observance and imaginative artwork, such as cave painting and figure molding, bead making, burying of the dead, and even musical instruments are in their infancy. Language is becoming prevalent. Tool-making with stone, wood, and creeping plant vines is widespread. Faint, but definite, signs of abstract thinking are just starting to show the hints of emergence.[8]

Between 7.6 – 6 TYA (5600 – 4000 BC), much of Mesopotamia shares a common culture, called the Ubaid culture, a derivative of the Sumerian civilization [9](named after the site where evidence for it was first found),[10] characterized by a distinctive type of pottery.[11] This historical era is called the Ubaid Period. The culture actually originated on the flat alluvial plains of southern Mesopotamia (ancient Iraq) around 6200 BC. About 5 million humanoids are living on the earth at this time. It is during this period that the first identifiable villages develop in the region,[12] where people farm the land using irrigation, and fish the rivers and sea.[13] This culture has for the first time a clear tripartite social division between intensive subsistence peasant farmers, with crops and animals, tent-dwelling nomadic pastoralists dependent upon their grazing herds, and hunter-fisher folk, living in reed huts. It is a fairly egalitarian society at first (although this markedly decreases over time), where social ranking is not very important.

The Ubaid culture is characterized by large village-type settlements, with multi-roomed rectangular mud-brick houses, and by the appearance of the first temples of public architecture in Mesopotamia. These villages contain specialized craftspeople, such as potters, weavers, and metalworkers, although the bulk of the population are agricultural and pastoral workers. Use of the plough and domesticated animals are hallmark features. Most commoners are farmers living outside the village walls. Everyone else lives within the village walls, including the rulers/overseers, priests and priestesses, traders, and slaves. Religion is very important to them. Like most cultures from ancient history, they are polytheistic, believing in and worshipping several nature-gods at once. They believe that the gods control everything, and that keeping them happy is of utmost importance.

It is within this culture and time that the Adam and Eve beings make their storied appearance. By this time, proto-humans had already dispersed throughout most of the earth. God then reveals himself with special favor and intention to a pair of highly developed creatures we know as Adam and Eve – real people with a high level of consciousness,[14] sentience,[15] and sapience,[16] whom God has selected as iconic 'avatars' for the rest of humanity.

Our Understanding of the Human Beginning

YA = years ago; K = thousand; M = million

- **First lemur-like primates, monkeys** (~ 55 MYA)
  (with an animal soul)
- **First Apes** (~ 33 MYA)
- **First Hominids** (~ 15 MYA)
- **First Human-like creatures** (upright-walking) (~ 8 MYA)
  - **Ardipithecus** (~ 5.8 MYA)
  - **Australopithecus** (~ 4.2 MYA)
- **Human-like creatures of genus Homo-**
  - **Homo-habilis** (~ 2.8 MYA)
  - **Homo-erectus** (~ 1.8 MYA)
  - **Homo-heidelbergensis** (~ 600 KYA)
  - **Neanderthals** (~ 400 KYA)
  - **First Homo-sapiens** (~ 200 KYA)
    (with a rational soul)
    - **Anatomically modern variants** (~ 160 KYA)
    - **Behaviorally modern variants** (~ 50 KYA)   *Upper Paleolithic Revolution (the Great Leap Forward)*
      (with an advanced rational soul)
      - **Cro-Magnon man** (~ 40 KYA)
    - **Behaviorally modern gracile variants** (~ 12 KYA)
      (modern sedentary Human Beings)
    - **First Human Beings in the 'Image of God'** (~ 8 KYA)
      (with more advanced rational soul + immortal ethereal spirit)

Adam and Eve

Note: Built-in to the design of human evolution is the
accommodation for Devine Intervention at many
times and places. But exactly when, where, and how   = Devine Intervention
all Interventions occurred is forever hidden from us.   for design adjustment

NOTES

1. The theory of abiotic synthesis proposes that life originated from non-living molecular compounds. It is also known as chemosynthetic theory because it suggests that life arose gradually from the synthesis of non-living organic molecules. But exactly how the 'soup' of organic molecules was created is another mystery. What must be available are the presence of building block molecules, energy, lack of free oxygen (the condition of the early earth's atmosphere), and time. Popular scenarios for producing the energy include comets/asteroids striking the early earth, radiation, atmospheric lightning, volcanic activity, non-volcanic deep-sea hydrothermal vents, and mud volcanism. The last two scenarios are particularly interesting in that hydrogen, methane, and hydrogen sulfide gases resulting from the thermal process driving the phenomena can provide the energy sources for chemosynthesis in the deep sea or mantle (without photosynthesis). Formation of these phenomena has been postulated to arise from the process of serpentinization, a non-biological geological low-temperature metamorphic process involving heat and water, in which low-silica igneous magnesium/iron rocks are oxidized and hydrolyzed into serpentinite (a dark, typically greenish rock, consisting largely of serpentine group minerals, such as antigorite, lizardite, and chrysotile, and composed of olivine/chrysolite and pyroxene). The process is highly exothermic and temperatures can be raised by about 500 °F. Observed methane traces found on Mars have been proposed to have been caused by serpentinization.

2. 600 cc = 36.6 cubic inches approx.

3. 1500 cc = 91.5 cubic inches approx. – of course, the average size is smaller, around 1200 cc, or 73 cubic inches.

4. From the anthropometric standpoint, some scientists think that consciousness occurs when the two halves of the brain become fully interconnected and integrated.

5. The pineal gland is a small endocrine gland in the brain of vertebrate creatures. It produces melatonin, a hormone which has various functions in the central nervous system, the most important of

which is to help modulate sleep patterns in both circadian and seasonal cycles. Melatonin production is stimulated by darkness and inhibited by light.

The shape and size of the gland make it resemble a pine nut; hence its name. The gland is located in the epithalamus, near the center of the brain, between the two hemispheres, tucked in a groove where the two halves of the thalamus join.

From the point of view of biological change, the pineal gland represents a kind of atrophied photoreceptor. In some lizards, sharks, bony fish, salamanders, and frogs, it is linked to a light-sensing organ, known as the parietal eye, which is also called the pineal eye or 'third eye'. It doesn't actually 'see' like a regular eye, but is instead just photoreceptive to light. It is sensitive to movement and the changes in light that occur when something moves through the environment above it.

The melatonin secretion of the pineal gland is only partially understood by science. Its location deep in the brain suggested to early philosophers that it possessed particular importance. This led to its being regarded as a 'mystery' gland with metaphysical, mystical, and occult theories surrounding its perceived functions.

17th century philosopher and scientist René Descartes regarded it as 'the principal seat of the soul'. Descartes split the human being into a body and a soul, and maintained that the soul was joined to the body by the pineal gland.

In the late 19th century, Madame Blavatsky (who founded theosophy) identified the pineal gland with the Hindu concept of the 'third eye', or the Ajna chakra. This association is still popular today.

6. The ability to perceive, reason, and thereby respond to selected features of the environment, and of interaction with other beings, is considered evolutionary by secularists. More ancient still, primitive awareness and primary consciousness appeared in the higher order animals and hominins – which may have been evolutionary, or gifted by God through divine intervention.

7. The species of bipedal primates, to which modern humans belong, is characterized scientifically by having a brain capacity of 1400-1500 cc (85-91 cubic in.), by dependence upon language (fostered by a

larynx), and by the creation and utilization of complex tools (fostered by agile/deft/nimble hands and fingers).

8. To feel, empathize, and accordingly respond to features of the environment, and to interact with other beings, in a reasoned manner – also called phenomenal consciousness, subjective consciousness, secondary consciousness, or intentionality – become behaviorally apparent. This may include the capacity to think about, and therefore conceptualize, one's own thoughts – to be self-aware and self-conscious.

9. Sumer was the southernmost region of ancient Mesopotamia (modern-day Iraq and Kuwait) which is generally considered the cradle of civilization. The name comes from Akkadian, the language of the north of Mesopotamia, and means 'land of the civilized kings'. The Sumerians were the people of southern Mesopotamia whose civilization flourished from 4100 to 1750 BC approximately, although early settlers are thought to have arrived as early as 6500 BC. No one knows where the Sumerians came from (after leaving Africa, they may have arrived directly by way of Arabia or Egypt, or indirectly by way of Europe or Persia), but by 2900 BC, they were firmly established in southern Mesopotamia. The first Sumerian cultural era is defined as the Ubaid Period, which lasted from roughly 6500 to 3800 BC.

10. Tall al-Ubayd (also spelled Tell el-Ubaid) is the ancient site that gave its name to this prehistoric cultural period. It is located near the ruins of ancient Ur in present-day southeastern Iraq.

11. A pottery style using loop handles and spouts, with black geometric lines drawn on a buff-colored body.

12. Some villages slowly began to develop into towns, and eventually people became focused on building large-scale construction projects, such as at Eridu and Uruk.

13. The Persian Gulf extended much further north at this time.

14. Heightened awareness, reasoning, will, and symbolic consciousness – these are traits that enable an individual to perceive,

reason, and respond to selected features of the environment, and to rationally interact with other beings – note that it is likely that primitive awareness and elemental consciousness were given to some of the higher order animals and hominins even earlier.

15. Sentience is the capacity to feel, empathize, and relate to the environment, and with other beings in a reasoned and shared manner – sometimes also called phenomenal consciousness, subjective consciousness, secondary consciousness, or intentionality – note that this may include the capacity to think about, and therefore conceptualize, one's own thoughts – to be self-aware and self-conscious.

16. Sapience is the cognitive basis for judgment, moral sentiment, strategic thinking, and system perspective – it integrates emotions, moral/social drives, intelligent decision-making, and creativity.

APPENDIX C

COMPUTER - CELL ANALOGY

Our knowledge about the inner workings of biological data and information processing is very limited. What we do know is that data processing in living organisms uses networked systems of biologically derived molecules – such as DNA, RNA, proteins, and cells - to perform logic calculations involving the storing, retrieving, and processing of data and information.[1]

The structure and function of all living things follows an organizational hierarchy. The levels in this hierarchy are molecules, cells, tissues, organs, systems (organ systems), and whole organisms. The organs and systems of the body help to provide all the cells with their basic needs to carry on the life functions. The cells of the body are of different kinds and are grouped in ways that help their function. But at each level, data and information processing occurs.

The organization and complexity of living beings is based on a coding system within the DNA-molecule. The natural function of DNA is to store hereditary information and regulate the distribution and use of this information. The directions for assembling the protein parts of cells and organs in the correct sequence and timing, is called the 'software of life'. These directions are information that is encoded into our DNA, using a digital code similar to binary computer code – but is quaternary instead of binary (using 4 symbols instead of 2) – that can be executed, much like a running program following a language protocol. Information stored in the DNA is encoded by way of various arrangements of four molecules called nucleotides –adenine, guanine, cytosine and thymine. These molecules are arranged in chains bonded together into what is called a 'double helix', which looks like a ladder that has been twisted into a corkscrew shape. Because of this, the DNA is very suited as a medium for data processing. Just as with binary computer code, this structure can store vast amounts of information for the execution of the protein assembly programs, as well as other programs. DNA computing is a form of parallel computing, in that it takes advantage of the many different molecules of DNA to try many different possibilities at once.

Biological Logic

What we know about DNA and DNA-based logic:

1) the order of nucleotides is used to store information (similar to memory)
2) recombinational behaviors reflect a higher order coding (like a formal language)
3) self-assembly behavior due to Watson-Crick base paring is algorithmic (like a logic computation)

What we know about RNA-based logic:

Input/output switching, and combinatorial logic (similar to electronic AND/OR/NOT gates), is implemented by the modification of RNA sequences. This is involved in regulatory networks.

What we know about protein-based logic:

Logic is implemented by the regulation of protein functions governing the production, destruction, localization, and behavior of biochemical molecules. This is involved in the crucial role of input and output information processing in the cell.

What we know about cell-based logic:

Intercellular signaling (cell-to-cell communication) can be used to build higher-order logic into biological systems. All basic logic gates are implemented in independent single cells that can then be networked together to perform complex logic functions.

The Biomolecular Computer

All living things are composed of one or more cells, each capable of carrying out the life functions. Inside each living cell are vastly complex molecular machines made up of various protein parts. Therefore, the cell can be thought of as a biomolecular computer – a dynamic information-processing system that responds to, and interacts with, a varied and changing environment. It represents a level of complexity that is orders of magnitude greater than the most sophisticated digital computer system. The cell is the basic building block of structure and of function in all living things. It gets information from its DNA by copying some base pairs from DNA to messenger-RNA. Cells have the potential to compute, and distribute the computational results both intracellularly and intercellularly (using cell-to-cell communication).

Higher order living things carry out the life processes of digestion, respiration, circulation, excretion, locomotion, immunity, coordination, and synthesis. These processes result from the execution of DNA programs, but the programs are so sophisticated that the instructions need to be distributed over many cells that are networked together.[2]

Numerical Complexity

Estimates for the number of cells in the human body range between 10 trillion and 100 trillion. Estimates for the number of nerve cells (those cells most proficient at data processing) range from 80 billion to 100 billion, or about the same as the number of stars in the Milky Way galaxy.

Furthermore, it is estimated that there are about 225,000,000,000,000,000 (225 million billion) interactions between cells (given the different cell types and cell features – neurotransmitters, neuromodulators, axonal branches, dendritic spines), and that doesn't include the influences of dendritic geometry, or the approximately 1 trillion glial cells which may be important for neural information processing.

So, it is clear that a higher order complex organism, like the human being, has the built-in computational and data processing capability to run complex algorithmic logic programs.[3]

Comparison with Silicon-based Data Processing

A common feature of both silicon-based data processing systems (a digital computer) and cell-based data processing systems (a lifeform) is the existence of a dedicated and distinct centralized information storage and processing (IS&P) complex.

In a silicon-based data processing system, the IS&P complex is divided into hardware and software facets.

The hardware facet consists of the processor (or microprocessor) computer chip (the central processing unit [CPU], consisting of gates, registers and logic circuits), the hard-disk drive or solid-state disk drive (including the interface circuits), RAM (Random Access Memory), ROM (Read-Only Memory), system controllers, and Input/Output (I/O) peripherals. The function of the CPU is intimately tied to its ISA (instruction set architecture), which defines how it will actually execute a program.

The software facet consists of the BIOS (basic input/output system) instruction set, the Operating System, and the application programs. A formal language enables the Operating System and application programs to be easily coded.

The hardware and software facets work together to implement the functional blocks of Input/Output, an Arithmetic Logic Unit (ALU), a System Control Unit (SCU), and Memory.[4]

In a cell-based data processing system, the IS&P complex is also divided into hardware-like and software-like facets.

The hardware-like facet consists of the physical DNA genetic material, gene expression molecular machinery, and the physical components of the cell (Golgi apparatus, proteins, enzymes, etc.). The general architecture and spatial organization of the cell, and the effect of the spatial configuration on the manifestation of biochemical laws, can be viewed as analogous to a silicon computer's ISA.

The software-like facet consists of the informational content of its genome sequence (the specific pattern of nucleic acids). Those aspects of the DNA sequence that code for the structure and function of the molecular machinery of DNA replication, RNA transcription, and protein assembly through translation, can be viewed as analogous to a silicon computer's BIOS and Operating System (this is sometimes called the 'software of life'). A language that enables the coding of the BIOS and Operating System is inherent in the sequencing of the DNA.

The hardware-like and software-like facets work together to implement functional operations between the genetic information encoded in the cell's DNA and its intracellular information-processing infrastructure (encoded in the RNA and proteins).

Analogies

Comparing a natural cell-based data processing unit with a man-made silicon-based data processing unit, is not an easy proposition. But if one insists on doing so, the following very loose analogies can be made:

DNA <==> computer code in semiconductor silicon

Golgi Apparatus <==> computer processor (CPU)

Nucleolus + Nucleoplasm <==> CPU chip socket

Endoplasmic Reticulum <==> RAM and the CPU bus (front-side bus)

Ribosomes <==> integrated circuit transistors in CPU chip

Nucleus <==> housing for main memory and CPU

NOTES

1. Information is organized data – contextualized, categorized, condensed, and patterned in some way so as to add value to the data, by making it more readily usable (manipulatable) in desired applications.

2. Examples of interdependent interaction networks are gene-regulatory networks, biochemical networks, transport networks, and carbohydrate networks.

3. Some would even say that the human being has been specifically designed to have the capability to run complex algorithmic logic programs.

4. Power supply and distribution is a related functional block that has been ignored for simplicity in illustrating the data processing loop. However, it is accommodated organically in the cell. The mitochondria take energy and store it for the cell to use (through a process called cellular respiration). Both the mitochondria and the power supply unit of a computer turn the energy that was captured from an external source and make it usable for the cell or computer.

About the Author:

Edward N Brown is a writer, researcher, and storyteller with a background in science, philosophy, ancient history, and theology. His technique is to blend the interesting nuggets of fact, drama, legend, mystery, romance, and spirituality – and mix them together into informative, but easy-reading, faith-based accounts of courage and heroism. An educational background of three advanced degrees (PhD + two MS) has contributed to his insights on Technology, Antiquity, Christianity, Morality, and Human Nature. Whether classified as Fiction or Nonfiction, his works represent an elegant fusion of style – action, dialog, thoughts, and depictions in riveting story form – excitement and intrigue that will inform, entertain, and inspire readers of all ages.

Other Books by Edward N Brown:

Simon vs. Simon: The Saint and the Sorcerer
The Missionary and The Magician
The Passion of Nino – the Enlightener
Passion of the Slave Girls
Saint, Martyr, Virgin, Slave: Faith and Freedom Forever
The Passion of Thecla: Faith and Fortitude
The Passion of Eve: Remembering the End
The Passion of Eve: Remembering the Beginning
  Revised Edition 2020

"I AM the ALPHA and the OMEGA," says the Lord God,
"the One Who is and Who was and Who is to come,
the Almighty!"
"I AM the ALPHA and the OMEGA, the First and the Last,
the Beginning and the End!
Blessed are they who wash their robes so as to have free
access to the Tree of Life ..."

Revelation 1:8 and 22:13-14

www.ingramcontent.com/pod-product-compliance
Lightning Source LLC
Chambersburg PA
CBHW060301050426
42448CB00009B/1718